# Lillian To

# Feng Shui Success Secrets

## Questions & Answers from Aunt Agga

COLLINS & BROWN

First published in Great Britain in 2000
by Collins & Brown Limited
London House, Great Eastern Wharf, Parkgate Road
London SW11 4NQ

Distributed in the United States and Canada
by Sterling Publishing Co.,
387 Park Avenue South, New York, NY 10016, USA

1 3 5 7 9 8 6 4 2

British Library Cataloguing-in-Publication Data:
A catalogue record for this book
is available from the British Library.
ISBN 1 85585 844 4

Consultant Editor: Liz Dean
Design: Jerry Goldie Graphic Design
Artworks: Susan Hellard

Reproduction by Global Colour Ltd, Malaysia
Printed by Dai Nippon Printing Co. Ltd, Hong Kong

Visit Lillian and Jennifer Too's world-famous feng shui online
magazine at: http://www.wofs.com

Or if you are interested in Buddhism, meet Lillian Too's Lama at:
http://www.lamazopa.com

Send feng shui e-greeting cards to all your friends and loved ones from:
http://www.fsgreetings.com

And visit the exciting and brand new world of feng shui megamall for
all your feng shui needs:
http://www.fsmegamall.com

# Contents

# 1

# Feng Shui Basics

## GETTING STARTED

T his is where you find out what you know –
and what you don't. The hundreds of e-mails I
receive every day are from beginners who seek
clarification on feng shui fundamentals without having to
read pages of Chinese philosophy. Here's where you find the
answers about those sometimes simple, sometimes tricky
first steps that will get you boosting your chi and removing
blockages to success. From how to pronounce feng shui to
that never-ending dilemma of the negative effects of fresh
flowers, televisions and water in the bedroom, all you need
do is read on, test your knowledge – and enjoy learning
from other peoples' trials and errors.

*Aunt Agga*

# How do I pronounce feng shui?

*Can you please tell me the correct pronunciation of "feng shui"? Is it feng "shwee" or "shway" or something? I do not know how to pronounce the "u" and "I". Anonymous*

Dear Anonymous

It doesn't really matter, but the correct way to say it is "foong schway".

# Can feng shui help improve my sleep?

*My friend introduced me to Lillian's books a couple of months ago and I have not stopped reading them since. My life has been completely rearranged. I have divided my apartment into the compass directions and my front door is split in half between the north and north-east directions. My KUA number is 4, making those directions my very best and my very worst! How do I get around that? Also, I have just started a job that relies heavily on commission, so I have moved my bed so that it faces north. In doing so my bed is put at an angle. I feel disoriented when I sleep and since then every night I have had strange, disturbing dreams. Am I doing the right thing? Anonymous*

Dear Anonymous

Well, you are an east person and it is important for you to determine very accurately whether the front door is facing north or north-east. In compass-formula feng shui there is a need to be accurate. So please note that you should get a good compass to take the measurement reading again. Since you want to do well in your new job, you might want to consider activating the north with a water feature such as an aquarium? As for your sleeping direction, my advice is to sleep with a solid wall behind you and use the sitting position to energize your sheng chi direction.

# Compass points

*How necessary is a compass in feng shui practice? Maggie*

Dear Maggie

Very necessary indeed, especially in the practice of compass feng shui. You should never rely on guesswork to establish your orientations. Invest in a compass and take the reading several times to be accurate.

# Clock–watching

*I bought a round wall-clock made out of cherry wood, and the size is about 30cm. (12in.) in diameter. Where is the best place to hang the clock? What does a clock represent in the feng shui world? Anonymous*

Dear Anonymous

A clock (or a watch) always represents the passing of time. It is not regarded as a good-fortune symbol, since it suggests growing older and is the antithesis of longevity. So hang clocks in unimportant corners and where they are not too obvious. Do not give watches as birthday gifts and definitely never give a watch to a family patriarch for his birthday.

# What's a "missing corner"?

*What is a "missing corner", and how do I know if I have one? Many thanks. Anonymous*

Dear Anonymous

If you draw a square or rectangle, and superimpose it over the plan of your house layout, you will see if there are any corners that are missing.

# A nightmare of a bedroom

*I'm moving to a new apartment and the master bedroom is a feng shui nightmare. The bedroom door is in the middle of the north wall. The whole east wall has mirrors, the west wall has a window, and the only solid wall is the south wall. The only walls I can put the head of the bed against are either the south or the west. If I put it against the west wall, I have a window at the head of the bed (bad feng shui, and unsafe, as I live in California and the glass could shatter during a tremor), plus the foot of the bed faces the mirrored closets of the east wall.*

*The south wall would be a good choice, but I cannot avoid having the foot of the bed (whole or partial) facing the main bedroom door. To counteract this I could put a divider screen at the foot of the bed. But since space is a little tight, could I get a canopied four-poster bedframe and hang a decorative sheet of cloth at the foot part of the bed, to act as a screen? If this is acceptable, can the cloth be a lace material, or does it have to be opaque? Thank you! Anna*

My very dear Anna
    Congratulations. You are systematic and logical in your use and analysis of feng shui. Your bedroom is not a feng shui nightmare. Everyone wanting to feng shui their room faces the same type of dilemmas that you have identified. Your analysis is correct, and your solutions are clever and practical. You are right – use the south wall and invest in a canopied bed. And no, the material need not be opaque.

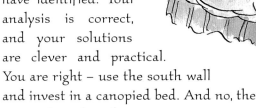

## Where should I hang a cross?

*My partner is a Christian and he would like to hang a brass cross in the house. According to most feng shui practices, a cross is a bad thing because it represents or creates "shar chi" (poison arrows). This cross has a special meaning to him, and I truly respect that. Where should I hang this cross? Terry*

Dear Terry
    To Christians the cross is a holy object with great significance and, as such, it is a symbol to be revered in a Christian household. In a way, the cross is to Christians what the Pa Kua is to the Chinese, in that it can be used to overcome shar chi or bad energy. So why not hang it at a special altar which you can create for your partner. Then place it in the north-west corner or against a north-west wall. By creating this special place for the cross it will bring you plenty of heaven luck. This is because the north-west is associated with heaven and divine practices of a spiritual nature.

# Watch out for charlatans!

*My interest in feng shui started only half a year ago and I try to practise it in every way I can. However, just this morning I came across an article that made my compass points spin out of control... it said that to downplay my negative direction I should place opposing elements/colours in that direction. I am a water rat, KUA 8. South is one of my negative directions, so it recommended that I place water objects here. I have been placing water objects in the north (universal career direction) all this time! I have swapped my red tissue box with the water jug now, but feel very uneasy as I don't know whether it is right or what the principle is behind it. Please enlighten me, Aunt Agga. Thank you very much. Sincerely, Lily*

Dear Lily

Please don't be so easily affected by people who write about feng shui in "bits and pieces". What you read in the article is, of course, nonsense and is clearly the viewpoint of a charlatan whose knowledge of feng shui is just too shallow. People do tend to mix up personal elements and directions with that of the environment or living space. So do not be influenced by articles that cannot give sound logical reasoning or any basis for what they recommend. Please go back to activating your north corner with water. As a rat, you will benefit hugely from water in the north, as this is enhancing your element. As for the south, putting water here will "put out the fire of recognition". Your good name and that of other residents in your home could be negatively affected with water in the south!

# Opposing theories

*I really enjoy your website with its good suggestions about feng shui. I have a question regarding the direction of my home. I have read multiple feng shui books, and there seems to be two theories: one suggests using the back of the house to face the right direction, and another advises that it's the front of the house that needs to face the right direction.*

*Lillian Too indicates the use of the back door of the house to face a good direction. This is what is called the Eight Directions Theory used by the compass formula. The same book describes the use of the front* door of the house to face a good direction: this is known as the Pa Kua Lo Shu formula. Could you please comment on these two theories and tell me which one I should follow? *Chang Lu*

Dear Chang Lu

Yes, in classical feng shui there are different formulas, which can be confusing and create dilemmas for the modern-day practitioner.

The two "theories" referred to in your question are considered together in a more advanced formula. For amateur practitioners, the recommendation is to use the KUA formula (also known as the Eight Mansions Formula) and try to orientate your front door according to one of your four good directions. Now, even in this KUA formula, one can go deeper and fine-tune the directions by considering what is known as the 24 mountains of the Eight Directions. As you go deeper into feng shui, you will definitely come across apparently contradictory recommendations. It requires much study to understand the nuances.

So unless you want to be a professional consultant and thus go deeper, my advice is to stay at the amateur practitioner's level and benefit from the simple and easy KUA formula. Feng shui does not have to be difficult or very profound for it to work!

## Solutions for mirror-tiles

We have just moved into a rental property, and in the entrance on the wall opposite the door are mirror-tiles. What can we do to stop the good chi from leaving? I have put a potted plant in front of the mirrors. Will this help? Could you please let me know what else I should do?
*Anonymous*

Dear Anonymous

You're on the right track. If you cannot remove the mirror-tiles facing your front door, covering them up would be the next best thing. A plant is excellent, because it helps the good chi that enters your house to meander gently into your home, rather than being bounced right out again. If you want to do more, you could also cover the mirror-tiles completely, perhaps with canvas? If you use suction pads to attach the canvas to the mirrors, it will not damage the tiles and your landlord won't be angry with you.

# Where do I put the three-legged frog?

*I have one quick question, if you don't mind. Firstly, I read in one of your many books that the three-legged frog is to be kept across the room from the front door and inside a cabinet or under a table. Then I found information saying the frog has to be near (but not directly in front of) the main door and face the door. Somewhere else said that it cannot face the door at all! Please let me know which of the above is correct. Thanks and my best regards to you, Avid Learner*

Dear Avid Learner

Actually the three-legged frog is just that. It hops around and goes everywhere, but for it to bring gold into the home, it should: a) be inside the house, b) not look as if it is about to go back out again, and c) appear to want to make a permanent home in your house. So it can face anywhere and be placed anywhere. Lillian Too has nine of these frogs placed all over her living room. Talk about overdoing things, huh? Like the Duchess of Windsor once said, "One cannot be too rich or too thin!"

# Glaringly difficult neighbours

*Recently my neighbour opposite hung a rectangular mirror with some Chinese writing in red ink on top of their main door. Can you tell me what this means and whether it affects us? I feel uncomfortable, as each time I walk out of my main door I feel the glare of the mirror in my eyes and find this rather irritating. Please advise what I should do. Anonymous*

Dear Anonymous

Oh dear, what an unfriendly neighbour! Please check if there is something about your house that might be disturbing your neighbour. If not, maybe you should ask her to remove the mirror... if she refuses you can hang a small Pa Kua mirror above your own front door, aimed directly at her mirror. This should, however, be a last-resort solution. If you have the space, better to plant a bushy tree to block off your neighbour's house. Otherwise you could inadvertently be starting a mirror war with your neighbour and this will only hurt both sides.

# Compass crisis

*I am quite desperate. Please tell me how to stand or face when holding the compass to find my auspicious locations. If I don't know this, how am I to be able to fix the feng shui of my house? Jenny*

Dear Jenny

The first thing to do is to understand your compass and learn how to tell where north is. Once you know where north is, you will be able to locate all the other directions.

It is important to understand the difference between the direction and the location. The direction is where you are facing. For example, you can be facing north or east, and you use the compass to tell you where north and east are and then you swivel round to face those directions. The location is the part of your home that represents the place of the direction. So if your front door is facing north, then the centre area around the front door would be the north location, and the immediate back of the house would be the south location. Once you have divided your home into the eight main compass locations, you can begin to identify the corners of your house; then, from your KUA formula, you can start to locate the corners that are auspicious or inauspicious for you.

# Can feng shui help my gay friend?

*After reading a section in one of your books on visualizing a partner, I was lucky enough to meet a wonderful man, whom I have now begun dating. Only a week in between!! Wow! There is one thing I need help on. I have a dear, sweet best friend (male and gay). I would love to help him with meeting a partner, yet I don't know if it is appropriate for this type of relationship? I mentioned to him about the negative energy he gives off and told him about your recommendations for visualizing a partner. I hope this is fine, but could you advise me whether it is or not? With great respect and gratitude, Marjorie*

Dear Marjorie

Oh yes, feng shui works just as well for gays, as long as they are clear about what they want. The main thing is to ensure a balance of yin and yang energy. Thus guys who tend to be more yang should energize their apartment with more yin, and vice versa. Otherwise the chi is out of balance and this is not good. And for gay couples living together, because they belong to the same gender, the yin and yang balance must be addressed at all times, especially in the décor of the place where they live.

## KUA formula success

*I had to write in and say that feng shui works – and, to Lillian Too, your articles and books have helped me a lot. I have noticed a very real and significant difference in my business ever since I repositioned my consultation desk to face my success direction. I will be moving to a new house soon and it faces my best direction, too. I hope it will be success after success from now on. Thanks again, Dr Tee*

Dear Dr Tee

Thank you for writing to share your good experience of the KUA formula with us. This formula is simple to understand and use. Incorporating one's personal auspicious directions based on the KUA formula should thus be a basic component of any beginner's practice of feng shui.

## Is a pair of goldfish lucky?

*I am confused about goldfish! I have bought two real goldfish and am wondering if these will bring me luck? Also, can you use feng shui to win back love? Many thanks, Godfrey*

Dear Godfrey

A pair of goldfish to signify a pair of lovers? Yes, you can use feng shui to win back a love, but for how long I cannot promise. If the karma between the two of you is over, then it's over. When it comes to love relationships, heaven luck is much stronger than the earth luck of feng shui.

## Where do I stand to take a compass reading?

*How do we measure the facing direction of the house? Where do we point the compass? Mid-point of the main door? Thanks, I.T.*

Dear I.T.

Good question... Stand at the centre of the open door and look outwards. Hold the compass at stomach level and make sure that it is level, then read the compass direction that points straight outwards. This is the facing direction of the main door.

# Is it okay to sleep on the diagonal?

*If I cannot move my bed according to my four good directions, can I still sleep in a diagonal position, so that my head will point in one of my good directions? As my bed faces north-east, I sleep diagonally so that my head is pointing east, which is one of my good directions. Is this right? Please help. Lean Chu*

Dear Lean Chu

Yes, some feng shui masters recommend sleeping with the head diagonal to the bed and even diagonal to the whole room, in order to tap the best direction, but Lillian Too says that this can be destabilizing. So on balance, I would say it depends on how you feel.

# Chinese compass confusion

*I've just started taking a closer look at feng shui. What confuses me when I read about the subject concerns directions. In your column, when you mention north, for example, are you referring to the north direction of a Western compass or do you mean north in Chinese directions (south on a Western compass)? Regards, Tim*

Dear Tim

Oh dear...it is only a convention that the Chinese place south on top – on the ground, and in reality, we are all referring to the same north, using any Western-style compass. When we refer to north in feng shui, we are referring to magnetic north, as indicated on any Boy Scout's compass.

# Using the elements in feng shui

*I keep reading about elements and how important they are in feng shui practice. Would you please tell me how to identify these elements (e.g. what is big wood, small earth, etc.?) and how I can use them in my house. For example, if I want to get rich, how do I use the elements to help me? Jerry*

Dear Jerry

The five elements referred to in feng shui are wood, fire, earth, metal and water. According to feng shui, everything in the universe is categorized as one of these elements and has a cyclical productive and destructive nature. Many feng shui recommendations are based on this cyclical relationship between the elements. Each of the eight directions has a symbolic element, which is said to be the essence of the chi, or energy, of that direction. Feng shui practitioners must therefore learn these element associations off by heart, since a simple but very effective approach to feng shui is to activate the element of each direction in order to activate what that direction stands for. Look at the table below and you will discover that to enhance your wealth opportunities, you should energize the south-east corner with the wood element (i.e. plants). To energize for a healthy life you should also place a plant in the east. Got it? Now commit the following table to memory and you are well on your way to becoming an expert:

| Direction | Element | What it represents |
|---|---|---|
| North: | water | career luck |
| South: | fire | recognition luck |
| East: | big wood | health luck |
| West: | small metal | children luck |
| South-west: | big earth | relationship luck |
| North-west: | big metal | helpful patrons luck |
| South-east: | small wood | wealth luck |
| North-east: | small earth | wisdom and learning |

# Correcting poison arrows
# from open shelves

*I read that open shelves act like poison arrows and should be covered
up using cabinet doors. Rather than putting doors on such open shelves,
would putting some kind of cloth over the shelves serve the same
purpose? Or perhaps would pointing the shelves towards a window
help? Thanks, Dan*

Dear Dan

If you cover the shelves with cloth, this has the same effect as using
doors to cover the shelves. As long as you cannot see the shelves, and
they are not openly cutting you and sending you bad energy, you are
fine. And yes, if they face a window they would be sending their shar chi
outside, so that's fine, too. But whichever way your shelves are facing
it is safer to cover them up.

# Conflicting advice on TVs and dried flowers
# in the bedroom

*I have read several books on feng shui and they seem to say different
things. I am now wondering if it is okay to have a TV in the bedroom?
And what about dried flower arrangements? Thanks, Sindy*

Dear Sindy

TVs per se would be fine if they were not reflective. Unfortunately,
most TV screens are. Having a TV in the bedroom, if it reflects the
bed, can make the marriage crowded. By reflecting the bed, the mirror
introduces a third party into the marriage – hence you could lose your
husband. If you want to have a TV in the bedroom, I suggest that you
cover it up with a screen or cloth when it is not in use.

As for dried flowers, they give out a lot of yin energy, which can
cause members of the household to fall ill. Instead, you should decorate
your home with live, vibrant flowers. This brings yang energy into the
home, creating auspicious chi. Note, however, that you should never
display flowers in the bedroom, as the bedroom is a place of rest. Too
much yang energy in the bedroom can cause sleepless nights.

## Should I avoid living in Denmark?

*I'm a Malaysian, but live in Denmark. Someone told me to avoid living in Canada or Denmark because it's not good for me, as I'm a rabbit. My birth date was 11 March 1975. I think I'm a wood rabbit. Anonymous*

Dear Anonymous

I have never heard of such sheer utter rubbish! Does this person mean to say that everyone born in rabbit years cannot live in Canada? Come on, don't be so gullible!

## Can feng shui help me choose a cat?

*I just read your column advising a "wood" person not to get a "silver-coloured" car because metal kills wood. Would the same hold true for house pets? I am a wood person and am thinking about getting a silver-tabby cat. Would I be better off with a brown-tabby cat or perhaps a solid black cat (representing water)? Thank you for your advice, Evelyn*

My dear Evelyn

Oh dear me, next we will be using feng shui to differentiate people according to the colour of their skins... I don't think so, somehow, do you?

Please go ahead and get your silver-tabby cat and enjoy him in the knowledge that he will bring you lots of yang energy to energize your living space with auspicious chi.

# 2

# Getting it Right

## FINE-TUNING
## FOR ABUNDANCE

Putting feng shui principles into action in your home isn't always as easy as it may sound – particularly if you're plagued by too many doors, irregularly shaped rooms, or living with fixtures and fittings that can't be moved. So, you've found your south-west corner to energize for love luck and you've tried to move you bed so you sleep with your head pointing towards your best direction – but discover you now can't open your bedroom door. This chapter shows you how to personalize feng shui to make it work for you, so those negative features, from overhead beams to mirror tiles, can be neutralized with minimum effort.

## *Aunt Agga*

# I can't calculate my KUA number

*I am facing difficulties getting my KUA number. My birth date is 1 September 1966. My wife, Janet's, is 11 April 1968. My daughter, Serena's, is 5 October 1996. Can you kindly illustrate how you get the KUA number? Your examples in one book show that the last two digits should add up to a single digit. Well, what about my case where 6+6 = 12. My understanding is that 12-10 = 2. Thus my KUA number is 2. Is this correct? Anonymous*

Dear Anonymous

The secret is to keep adding the numbers until you reduce them to a single digit. So for you (a male), add the last two digits of your year of birth, 6+6 = 12, and then 1+2 = 3. To get the KUA number, deduct this from 10, which gives you a KUA number of 7.

In the case of your wife, 6+8 = 14 and then 1+4 = 5. For her (a female) you then add 5, so 5+5 = 10 and then 1+0 = 1, so her KUA number is 1.

For your daughter, her KUA number is 2 – and I hope you know how I got this... If not, then you need to go back to school (only kidding).

# How do I fill a wealth vase?

*Could you give me some information on wealth vases: how full do you fill them with dirt, and how many semi-precious stones do you put in? Also, the only cupboard that I have in the east of my house has glass doors. Does the vase have to be in the dark, and where is the most auspicious place to have the vase? Anonymous*

Dear Anonymous

Wealth vases need to be hidden away, in that they should not be displayed in an obvious fashion, but should be kept inside your bedroom out of view of visitors. You can create a wealth vase by filling it with seven types of semi-precious stone, three-quarters full, to allow space for more wealth to come in. It should also contain some earth taken (with his permission) from a rich man's house; three coins tied with red string; and other symbols of wealth. These can be real money placed in an auspicious red packet, or some rice to symbolize always having plenty to eat; you can also place real gold and jewellery inside. It is a good idea each new year to "add to the wealth" inside the vase to symbolize growth in your assets.

# Feng shui is certainly not a religion

*My name is Cynthia and I am a feng shui beginner. My brother had been without a job for several months, but after I rearranged his apartment, not only did he get a job within three weeks but he has now been offered an even better job.*

*I have to confess that in the beginning I was sceptical about feng shui. As a staunch Roman Catholic, I am suspicious of anything "religious". But Lillian's book kept stressing more than once that, to her, feng shui does not involve religion. She even says, "It is better to put a person's individual religious symbol – be it Muslim, Christian or Buddhist – in the home facing the main door..." That really impressed me. My husband, who is usually a sceptic, has also not said anything against my interest, even though he too is a staunch Catholic. So I am now writing to seek help on some major feng shui problems in my home. Could you please advise me on these three questions:*

1.  *My entrance door is in line with my main gate. I have a large car porch and a driveway between the gate and the main door. I cannot change the position of my door and cannot place a partition (plants, etc.) between the gate and the front door, as the cars need to drive in straight. What shall I do ?*
2.  *The headboard of my bed in the master bedroom is facing the entrance door. It is also in line with the opening that leads to my walk-in closet which in turn leads to my bathroom. Unfortunately my bathroom does not have a door (but the toilet does not face the door opening). I cannot change the position of the bed, as I have a three-door window on one side and a bay window on the other.*
3.  *The gas stove in my kitchen is next to my sink. There is a concrete slab space before the actual sink, but it is still in line (fire and water). Also, my gas stove is almost (but not quite) directly in line with the toilet in my master bedroom upstairs. I cannot move the gas stove as it is built in. Can you kindly assist me in anyway? Thank you so very much, Cynthia*

Dear Cynthia

You will be happy to hear that your problems are not difficult to solve. Firstly, you are right about your main door being afflicted by poisonous chi caused by the straight driveway. Hang a windchime outside the door to transform the bad energy into good. Make sure that the rods are hollow and reasonably large. Secondly, change your bed position. Better to sleep with a window above the head than to have it pointed towards the door and the bathroom. Thirdly, move your stove from underneath the toilet to guard against illness and away from the sink. Although it is built in, the benefits of moving the stove are worth the expense of doing so.

# Hanging crystals correctly

*Where is the best place to hang a crystal: in a bedroom or a study room? How high should it be from the ceiling? Regards, Camellia*

Dear Camellia

Hang a crystal in the north-east of your study to enhance your wisdom luck, and in the south-west of your bedroom for relationship luck. Crystals should never be too high and I prefer to place them on table tops rather than hanging them. This is because crystals are of the earth element and are best when they are grounded.

## Aquarium under the staircase

*I have just read that having water under the staircase is not auspicious for my children's luck. In that case, can I relocate my aquarium to the south-west direction of my house? It will then be in the dining area as my living and dining room are combined. Belle*

Dear Belle

You should definitely remove the aquarium from under the staircase, but to move it to the south-west could cause problems, since the water element is not good for the earth element of the south-west. Instead why don't you try to find a niche for it in the north, south-east or east of your dining-cum-living area.

## Hanging windchimes

*My question is: if I hang a black five-rod, hollow metal windchime in the north-west direction, in accordance with your advice, is this windchime suitable to press down any bad luck? Michelle*

Dear Michelle

Yes, if the bad luck is in the east or south-east corner. In addition, the windchime is very effective in overcoming the Five Yellow affliction of Flying Star feng shui. The Five Yellow brings enormous bad luck and was in the north sector in the year 2000.

# Feng shui in a new workplace

*I wonder if you can help. My company has just moved into a new factory. I want to know, when referring to my personal directions, should I be referring to the main entrance of the building or to the entrance of my cubicle? I am also confused by your reference to magnetic north. Does that mean I don't have to bother where I face in order to get directions and that, wherever my compass points, that will be my north? Also, my back is facing the entrance of my cubicle (which cannot be helped), which is directly exposed to a window. Outside is a street light, followed by vacant land, then another factory and, in the distance, a mountain. I can control the blinds to the window. Can you please let me know if my current sitting position is okay? Should I leave the blinds open or closed? David*

Dear David

You must definitely use the compass to get your orientations. How else would you know where north or any other direction is? As to which entrance is significant in feng shui, my answer is both. The entrance into the building should face one of your good directions. If it does not, try and enter through a door that does. The entrance to your cubicle should also face a good direction. The mountain view from your window sounds pleasant, so leave the blinds open. To see if your sitting position is good for you, check that you are facing one of your good directions.

# Two doors in a row

*We recently bought a new house and, after reading your book, we realized that our main door faces the door leading to the children's room. Can we put an artificial plant there to draw the attention away? The double-decker bunk beds in the children's room are directly facing the door. We read that this is not good. Can we place a bookshelf at the end of the bed, so that the bookshelf faces the door? Chandrasekti*

Dear Chandrasekti

Having two doors one after the other causes chi to move too fast. But two doors in a straight line are less harmful than three doors in a straight line. By placing a plant between the doors you have hit on the ideal solution. Meanwhile, inside your children's bedroom, placing a bookshelf between the bed and the door will slow down the chi.

# Where do I put my fish tank?

*I am confused over where I should put the fish tank in my apartment. One book I read suggests that it is best to put it on the south-east side of the room; the other, based on my date of birth, says to put it on the north side (this is my bedroom location). Based on my spouse's date of birth, it would be best to put it on the south side. Please advise me. And can I use salt-water fish instead of goldfish? Please also advise me on where I should put my tortoise? Meredith*

Dear Meredith

There are always different options in the feng shui placement of auspicious features. The challenge is to find out which corner is the most auspicious. The south-east and north are generally good directions to place water features, but if this happens to be your bedroom, then even though these directions may be auspicious, water in the bedroom is not. As for putting water in the south, well I have never heard of this being good, unless the Water Star here according to the Flying Star formula is auspicious. Certainly this is not due to the date of birth. So you must weigh up your options and then decide where is the best place for you.

As for keeping salt-water fish, this is up to you. Auspicious fish, according to feng shui, are the goldfish, the carp and the arrowana. The tortoise is best placed in the north.

# Getting round the lunar calendar

*I just need to check with you regarding how to calculate the "KUA". Lillian Too's book says that the formula should use the lunar calendar year of birth, so how do I know how to determine this? I am a Westerner born in Scotland and we do not have the lunar calendar here. Please help. Anonymous*

Dear Anonymous

The difficulty with the lunar calendar is that the New Year date varies each year, so one needs the whole 100-year calendar in order to determine the exact date of cut-off when converting Gregorian dates of birth to the Chinese calendar. However, I am told that if you use 4 February as the cut-off date, this should be acceptable. Thus, if you were born before 4 February, you should deduct one year from your year of birth before applying the KUA formula.

## Cactus plant in the corridor

*My neighbour placed a big cactus plant along our common corridor in the path of my front door. Is there any way to defect the shar chi? Thank you, Helen*

Dear Helen

As the cactus is outside your apartment and in the common corridor, it acts as a protector for your home. Cacti are only harmful when they are inside the house, because the thorns then create secret poison arrows. Outside they become a protective symbol.

## How can I avoid bad fortune on a wedding day?

*I know you are a very busy woman, but I sincerely hope that you can help me. My niece is getting married on a "rabbit" (mao) day, which clashes with the earthly branch of my year of birth (1969: rooster). Under normal circumstances I would have avoided any major under-takings on a "rabbit" day. Unfortunately, I must attend the wedding (she's one of my favourite nieces). Are there any remedies that can help me to minimize the clash? Please help me. Anonymous*

Dear Anonymous

Hey, don't panic. Your niece is not going to get hurt if you attend her wedding. She probably will be hurt if you don't. This so-called clash of the earthly branch elements is a small matter. It might cause you to get a headache, but nothing more serious than that. If it will make you feel better, however, you might want to carry something metallic on your body – so wear lots of gold that day to overcome any bad vibes. That is all that is required. You now have an excuse to go to town on the jewellery!

# Determining door direction and location

*I notice that Lillian Too mentions two ways of selecting the direction for a house. One way is the Lo Shu square way and the other is by using the compass direction. Which is more accurate? For example, if I put the compass in the middle of my house, the whole front wall of the house is five degrees away from the actual north direction. Is this direction still considered north? Then, if I draw the nine squares, the whole front wall is divided into three squares, which become north-west, north and north-east. According to the Lo Shu grid this shows that my wooden door is on the north-west square, the window is on the north square and the sliding glass door is on the north-east square. Which north should I take? And should I consider the whole front wall or the window direction? Thanks and regards, Belle*

Dear Belle

Many people get mixed up between direction and location. In your case, your main door is said to be facing north but is located in the north-west. You see, when you take the direction with a compass, it tells you the orientation of the house. So whether you take the direction from the centre or the front, it will still show the same orientation. Compass directions do not change. But when you superimpose the Lo Shu grid on to the house plan, then you are using the orientation of the house to determine the different compass locations. So on the north orientation of a rectangular house the three grids of the front panel of the Lo Shu square will show north-west, north and north-east. Please note that your door can be located in any of these three grids and still face north. In feng shui, both location and direction are equally important.

# An over-abundance of windows

*Just one question – if I have too many windows in my house, does it help to have voile (clear curtains that you can see through), so that the chi does not come into the house and go straight out? Jerry*

Dear Jerry

When there are too many windows, chi moves in an inauspicious manner. Voile curtains are not enough, better to use heavier material.

# A satisfied reader

*I wanted to write to thank Lillian Too for her generosity in sharing her expertise in feng shui with us by writing all those books. They have changed our lives. My husband and I have moved to a house facing south (our best direction). Our rice cooker, stove, coffee maker, toaster and microwave oven are all facing south-east (our third best). I've placed my computer so that I sit facing my best direction, put a water feature in the south-east, paintings of arrowanas (nine) in the south-east, and our bathroom is in the north-east, as well as our kitchen. So far, so good! Before we moved I had no idea I would start a business, but within two weeks I had started one and it just exploded! I'm receiving so many leads I'm swamped! My e-mails went from one or two a week to 100 per day! Nothing compared to you, I bet, but ekkk! I'm just so excited and thrilled! Thank you, thank you, thank you! Estrella*

Dear Estrella
Nice to get such excellent feedback.

# Is a white wall a poison arrow?

*My main door faces a white wall that divides my house from my neighbour's. In your book you mentioned poison arrows hitting the main door. Is this wall bad? Should I hang a windchime between the main door and the wall? Mary*

Dear Mary
Your wall is certainly not a poison arrow. However, depending on how high it is the wall can be interpreted as a mountain. Hanging a windchime is a good idea if the wall represents the west or north-west.

# Pond on the left or on the right?

*Which is better for a pond in the garden if the right is the north: on the left-hand side of the door or on the right-hand side? Regards, Jenny*

Dear Jenny
On the right-hand side the pond brings more wealth, but here is also where the pond will cause your husband to develop a roving eye. So what do you want – more wealth and an unfaithful husband, or less wealth and a loving husband?

# Can water cures be substituted by crystal cures?

*About activating the north corner: can I use crystal instead of water? I came across an article about the application of crystal, and the author said that crystal belongs to the water element. Well, I'm quite confused. Anonymous*

Dear Anonymous

Not at all! Crystal belongs to the earth element. The confusion arises because some people look on crystal as frozen water! However, this is a Western concept and is not part of feng shui.

# What school of feng shui to follow?

*Please forgive my rather elementary question: living in the USA, I am trying to figure out what school of feng shui I should practise. I understand that the Black Hat Sect is quite popular here in the West, but if I follow this, the front door of my home (which faces south) would represent my career sector, while traditional Chinese compass-school feng shui says that my career sector is oriented to magnetic north (the rear of my home). I lean towards practising the traditional Chinese compass school because it is (as you know) based on a scientific approach thousands of years old. Please help me understand how one goes about making this decision, especially if choosing one method clearly means that the sectors of my home will be the opposite of those of the other school. Many thanks for the opportunity to ask you this question. I look forward to your reply, Carrie*

Dear Carrie

Well, well, aren't we feng shui enthusiasts lucky? Not only do we get to change and improve our luck with feng shui, but we get to choose from so many different methods to achieve our aims! But of course when one has too many choices, it sometimes poses a dilemma. When it comes to making such personal choices, you yourself must decide.

The Black Hat Sect is more well known in the USA because of the wonderful work done by Prof. Lin Yun in sharing his knowledge of feng shui. However, we practise a different way of superimposing the Pa Kua. We use the compass and have found this to work very well. Why don't you give this method a try and, if it works – well, there you have your answer.

## I'm confused over my elements

*I've got one question. There are some books on the market that talk about a person's destiny. This is based on the hour, day, month, season and year of birth. A person's element is also determined by this. Heaven stem and earth branch are involved. From this method I found out that I am a weak wood person.*

*Then I read Lillian Too's book and found that, based on my year of birth, I am an earth person. What I am most confused about is that the feng shui application is very different for the two different elements. So which should I follow? Other authors do not seem to talk much about application or solution, just about analysis. Siew Lan*

Dear Siew Lan

Destiny is fortune telling, based on the four pillars of one's birth – i.e. the hour, day, month and year – which then allows the expert to work out the stem and branch of each pillar, all of which have a matching element. Thus every person is said to have eight elements, and from this the practitioner will be able to tell you many things about your destiny. From this he can also tell you that you are a "weak wood person" and that there-fore you need water or fire, or some other element. Now it may be that in your year-pillar you have either the stem or the branch as an earth element.

If you think systematically like this there is no reason to be confused. Feng shui is not dependent so much on these personal elements, although yes, there are some systems that do rely on the person's elements. Lillian Too's books give you a step-by-step method to check your element and then to tell you how to use that information.

# 3

# Career Blues

## FINDING SUCCESS AND HARMONY AT WORK

We spend too long at work to be unhappily employed or even worse, unemployed. Judging by the number of questions I receive from people with career blues, we're all trying hard to get the best from our jobs. Whether you're striving to be the next MD of your company or going for a career makeover, feng shui can help you get what you need in business. Firstly, know where to sit for good fortune; next, remove blockages to success such as "poison arrow" open shelving; then enhance your career luck with energizers such as mountain symbols, fish, crystals and a feng shui business card. Your career may not be a disaster zone, like some in the following pages, but practising feng shui can make work really work for you.

*Aunt Agga*

# Out of work...what can I do?

*I was born on 10 November 1958. I am married and a father with four kids. I was holding a senior position in a company, but was made redundant (retrenched) a year ago and am currently unemployed. How am I going to overcome the problems? Please advise. Regards, Greg*

Dear Greg

Redundancy happens to the best of us and it can sometimes be the start of something even better in our careers. Take a positive attitude and systematically improve your feng shui at home. Firstly, check all your directions. Next, make certain that your door and your sleeping position are not being hurt by harmful objects. These are the basics of feng shui. I would not be surprised if, in your audit of the feng shui of your home, you discover the bad feature that caused you to lose your job. So stay cool and get started.

# Lawyer cannot find work since moving

*I am an environmental/energy law attorney who lives in the New York City Metro area and I can't find a position since we moved around 15 months ago. It seems that I get very close to being offered a job, and then boom...either the company is downsized, being sold off, moving its headquarters away or else I am "too senior" (translate this to mean "too highly paid") and someone younger and/or cheaper gets hired. I know that there is nothing wrong with my résumé, my credentials or how I interview. What can I do around my house (and where should these things be placed) to activate luck in the career, money and recognition sectors of my life? Anonymous*

Dear Jobless Lawyer

Hey, have you discovered my very powerful KUA formula? This is the formula that ensures that every individual knows his or her most auspicious direction. So start by getting your best directions and then systematically change your door, your bed, sleeping and sitting directions and locations. You will be amazed by how your luck will change almost immediately. Almost all my books carry this formula, so you only need get one of them for reference.

# Colleagues fight and my efforts are not appreciated

*We moved to a new office recently and lately there seems to be a lot of discontentment among office members. There have been a few unpleasant incidents where staff have passed angry remarks about each other, and I think I am not appreciated for the work I put in. The computers are in a fixed spot and it will not be possible for me to move or face a good direction. What shall I do? Please advise. Thank you, Tan*

Dear Tan

To start with, you can open up all the windows and let out the bad energy of the office. Next, place some fresh flowers on your desk to dissolve any surrounding chi that may be hurting you. Thirdly, look around you for sharp edges and above you for exposed beams. Make sure that no sharp, pointed or hostile edges are aimed at you. Then try to sit facing at least one of your good directions. Even with computers around you, you can still swivel your chair to face a good direction and this will ensure you are appreciated for what you do.

# Using feng shui enhancers at work

*I have a crystal ball, a pink quartz, a pointed, greenish-coloured stone (meant for career) and even a small turtle on my window sill in my office cubicle. It looks like I am obsessed with trying to improve my career. I am still having problems with colleagues and I don't think I have advanced much. My KUA number is 9. The window is on the north-east. The L-shaped table is along north-east and south-east. I use my notebook 90 per cent of the time. Which direction should it face? Please advise. Alexandra*

Dear Alexandra

In feng shui it is not how much you do, but how effective that one energizer or cure is. Feng shui is not just about placing auspicious objects; you need to put them in the right corners. In the wrong place they can do harm to the energy around you. In your case, Alexandra, my advice is to remove all those things from your window ledge and instead hang a single cut-crystal to catch the sunlight and bring in yang energy in the form of rainbows and lights. The turtle should be behind you, not on your window sill. Finally, sit facing either north, south, east or south-east, as you are an east person and these are your auspicious directions.

# Is the location of the door always the career corner?

*I am new to feng shui and totally confused as to the directions. I know where east, north, south and west are…but my girlfriend says that, depending on where the door to each room is, this determines where each sector will be. She claims that the door is always located in your career sector, but the more I read here, the more I think she is misin-formed. I could sure use some help in this department. Thanks, Pat*

Dear Pat

She is simply using the Black Hat Sect style of feng shui. This sect uses the door "to establish the career corner" and all other corners as well. Practitioners of real Chinese feng shui consider this method not to be authentic, of course, since the compass is central to the ancient Chinese practice of feng shui. I prefer to go with the compass. Once you under-stand the source of your confusion, you should no longer feel at odds.

# Tuition-centre feng shui

*I am currently running a tuition centre. Can you give me some tips to improve business and make it auspicious for any students who learn with us? Can I use the "knot without end" as the logo for the centre? Currently our logo features three people under a graduation cap (a guy in between two girls), but we're thinking of changing it. Also, can I hang portraits of famous scientists at the centre? Dorothy*

Dear Dorothy

The knot would be extremely unsuitable, as this is basically a love-and-marriage symbol. Your present logo is better, but if you add one more person it would be more balanced. Perhaps another guy. It is an excellent idea to hang portraits of scientists in your centre. This is one of the best feng shui tips. I remember that when Lillian wanted her daughter Jennifer to score double As in her maths and advanced maths papers in her pre-university A-level exams, she bought a portrait of Einstein and hung it in front of Jennifer's bed, so that each morning she woke up seeing the face of this mathematical genius. Needless to say, Jennifer did indeed succeed in getting her double distinctions for maths.

# Sitting with my back to a window

*I read in a book of feng shui by Lillian that I should always sit with my back to the wall. Well, where I work I sit facing the front entrance, looking west, with my back towards a copying machine and with a big window behind me and a door into the office on my left. Behind that glass window another employee sits. She can see just about everything I do from her desk through the window. So what can I do to help myself in this situation? Rubin*

Dear Rubin

Well, to start with, your window at least does not open on to an empty space outside, but instead only separates your office from your colleague's. If the person sitting behind you is your friend, or can help you, then the sitting orientation is good. If not, then it means that that person could betray you if an occasion of conflict arises. So my suggestion is for you to swivel your seat around so that you can at least see her. Otherwise, invest in a plant and place it behind you to create a block between you.

# What are the best career energizers?

*In the north corner of my living room I have a small table where I have placed the following items, hoping to activate and improve my career luck: a) five decorative ceramic tortoises, b) two small ceramic lions tied with red ribbons around their necks, c) a table lamp, d) a small decorative container with cover. They also serve as decorative ornaments for the living room. Are these items okay? Regards, Alvin*

Dear Alvin

You only need one tortoise. The ceramic lions should be placed at the two sides of your entrance door. You do not need a table lamp here in the north. You also do not need the decorative container. What would be great, however, would be a goldfish bowl with some happy goldfish swimming inside.

# Bedroom or study?

*I turned 27 years old on 4 April. My situation is that I live and run my business out of the basement of my parents' house (I am trying to pay off $34,000 in credit-card bills and also trying to bring in money for my business – I am a personal manager for recording artists).*

*The room in the basement where I work and sleep is a large, rectangular-shaped room. The dilemma I have is: I know that you do not recommend having water in the bedroom, but I have a fish tank there because it is also my office – I only sleep there in a sleeping bag that I roll up in the morning. Is this a case of water in the bedroom or water in the office that I sleep in? Sincerely, Rob*

Dear Rob

I take it that you live in a studio, where everything happens in the same room (work, sleep and more...)? Because if you do have another room that you

can energize, I suggest that you place your wealth-bringing water feature in the north of the living room. Avoid having water in the bedroom, even if you work there. What you could do is to face your best direction while working, and sleep with your head pointing towards your best direction. Or you could look for recording artists with more star quality to manage.

# Hotel room office

*What kind of water element is good for my new business? I'm currently running my office from a hotel room. I find that people do not trust or believe in my services. According to your book, it is advisable to put nine goldfish in a small tank to create energy. Is there anything else that I can put in the room so that my business will grow? Anonymous*

Dear Anonymous

Hey, listen, would you trust anyone doing business from a hotel room? You know what kind of people do business from there, huh? Now you may be the most bona fide, serious businessperson, but your feng shui is completely out of sync with the expectations of the world. It is better to do business from your home than from a hotel room. Believe me, all the goldfish in the world cannot help in this situation.

# I can't concentrate after moving to a new area of the office

*I would like your advice about a situation at work. I am a wooden dragon, date of birth 22 January 1965, and I live and work in Brisbane, Australia. I am currently the Manager of a Secretariat in the Federal Government. Recently our office had some renovations done and I moved to another part of the office. My new desk faces north. Since I have moved here I have had a lot of trouble concentrating and I can't seem to finish any of the policy papers I am writing. What seems to make this worse is that I have my back to the door. Anonymous*

Dear Anonymous

Oh dear, you must quickly do something about your office. Firstly, please do not sit with your back to the door. There is no cure for this. You simply have to change your sitting direction. Secondly, you should calculate your KUA number to see if your sitting direction is good for you. Based on your date of birth, your KUA number is 9 if you are male and 6 if you are female. Try to sit facing one of your good directions, which is of the east group if your KUA is 9 and of the west group if your KUA is 6. And by the way, you are a wood rabbit, not a wood dragon (you are definitely not concentrating). Make an effort to find out what your directions are.

## How do I improve my workspace?

*I am trying to improve my space at work to enhance my career. I am a KUA number 7, which suggests that I should face the west. If I do this, my desk will be directly facing and touching the wall of shelves in my area and I can't change where they are. At the moment I face east, with the shelves behind me. Anonymous*

Dear Anonymous

That's just as bad, so it would be better to move around and face west. Then go out at lunchtime and buy a white curtain to cover the exposed bookshelves. This should help you.

## Business cards

*I want to have a business card printed for my boyfriend as a gift. I am choosing black writing on white paper with an emblem of a Chinese dragon, as I have read that this will increase his good fortune. Is it possible that I could get this horribly wrong by choosing the wrong dragon or anything else? Please help! My gift has good intentions and I really want it to help him in his career. Julie*

Dear Julie

Your good intention is absolutely spot-on! The dragon image is a highly auspicious symbol, and black on white is a good colour combination. So good luck to you and your boyfriend. He is very lucky and already enjoys good fortune with such a nice girl like you.

# Help – I'm sandwiched between two toilets!

*To maximize my sheng chi, my desk in the office is positioned to face west (my direction), which makes it face a door. What makes it worse is that I am now sandwiched between two toilets (i.e. behind my chair is a toilet and facing the front is the main bathroom). Any tricks to deflect this unfortunate position? Your attention is very much appreciated. Sincerely, Pauline*

Dear Pauline

Feng shui is not a trick, and no, there are none that I can offer for your situation, except to advise you to move your desk out of the "line of fire" created by the invisible straight line between the toilet and the bathroom. Perhaps you should find another room.

## Coping with a fierce poison arrow

*My spouse works in a trading company and they have moved from the 58th floor to the 41st floor of the same building. When they moved to the lower floor, they realized that the sharp edge of a lower building was pointing directly at their trading floor, like a poison arrow cutting the trading floor in half. It is very clear, as the whole floor has glass panels. What can they do to rectify the bad chi from the sharp edge of the nearby building? Will pasting Sun-X film on the window panel divert the bad chi? Please advise. Andrew*

Dear Andrew

No, Sun-X film is no match for this very fierce poison arrow. Nor will puny little Pa Kua mirrors do much to help. What you need is to get two large stone lions or fu dogs, at least 1m. (3 ft.) tall, and place these on either side of the window, looking out at the edge. If this is not sufficient, then install a mirror on the window looking out, so that the big window-mirror reflects the edge back again and completely closes off the view of the building. I know this sounds drastic, but it is necessary. Otherwise the trading-room staff will get sick and eventually there might not even be a company left.

# Is it bad feng shui to sit under bright lights?

*My office work chair is located directly under the office lights, I can't move my chair and the table is immovable. What should I do?*
*Anonymous*

Dear Anonymous

What is your problem? Is it that the lights are too bright and harsh, thereby causing an excess of yang energy? If so, may I suggest that you make an effort to cool things down by wearing more blues and blacks in your clothes. If possible, place an urn of still water near your table to absorb the light energy.

# Where do I put my arrowana fish?

*I have read in Lillian Too's book that the arrowana be placed in the south-east sector of the house. But you recommend that they be placed in the north. So which is better or correct? Thanks, Bob*

Dear Bob

The arrowana can be placed in either the south-east or the north. Both are good, and both are correct.

The south-east is the universal wealth corner and is ruled by the element of wood. Water produces wood, so by placing your arrowana here, you are using an element energizer to activate the luck of this sector. The arrowana fish represent wealth, so you are further energizing the luck of that corner.

In the north sector, which represents career luck and is ruled by the element of water, you are energizing the luck of the corner directly by placing a water feature there. And if you want your money fish (your arrowana) to bring you wealth throughout your career, you are further energizing that corner.

Which is "better" will depend on external factors, such as Flying Stars in the north corner (e.g. nine and five which bring bad luck) and you place your arrowana there. By strengthening the north with water, as well as enhancing your career luck, you are actually strengthening your bad luck, too. There are always many aspects to think about when practising feng shui – and sometimes you cannot achieve the perfect solution. What you should aim for is the best feng shui you can get, given other unchangeable factors.

## Enhancing my personal career

*I am interested in improving my career and personal status at work. With KUA number 6, my sheng chi should be west. However, in my office cubicle, my table is L-shaped and is facing north-east, east and south-east, and my back is exposed. I am sitting facing north-east and I cannot change the table position to sit facing west. To make things worse, my department is in the basement of the building and we have exposed beams running all over the place. Putting up a false ceiling is out of the question, so is putting up flutes or camouflaging with plants. What else can I do so that they do not harm me? T.J.*

Dear T.J.

Tough luck – looks like you will have to live with those beams of yours. Seriously, you should move out of the way of the beam that is directly above you and invest in a light, which you should keep turned on throughout the day. Shine the light at the beam daily. Next, you must endeavour to sit facing at least one of your good directions. Now, while it may be difficult for you to do much about the feng shui at work, you can and should maximize your feng shui at home. Sit, sleep and work facing your sheng chi at home and you will benefit from your KUA directions.

# 4

# Health Hazards

## BOOSTING YOUR WELL-BEING

You can literally use feng shui as your personal house doctor. By curing "bad" energy in your home, you can enhance your chances of good health. As you will see in this chapter, health problems often go hand-in-hand with relationship glitches and even financial crises. Stress is frequently the culprit and living in an unbalanced environment where bad feng shui prevails can drain you of the energy essence that brings good health. Read on and discover the location of your health corner and health direction, and how activating it through simple feng shui techniques can boost you physically and mentally.

*Aunt Agga*

# Is there a feng shui cure for depression?

*Please help me. My father is slowly dying of depression. Ever since his retirement, he sits all day staring into space. He won't eat and he will not say anything. He just sighs and sighs. It breaks my heart to see him this way. Is there anything I can do to make him come alive again? He used to be such a happy man. My mum passed away many years ago, so I know it's not this. Janice*

Dear Janice

Yes, you could definitely use feng shui in this situation. Check his bedroom and infuse it with a dash of yang energy. Place a red lamp in the south and the south-west. This will create the chi that brings recognition and friends calling. Next, invest in either a stereo system or a pet (a dog?) for him. This brings in yang energy and will engage his mind. Lastly, work out his auspicious directions based on his date of birth and move his bed so that he sleeps with his head pointing in one of his good directions (preferably the nien yen direction). All these things should help to shake him out of his misery and probable loss of self-confidence. May I say what a kind daughter you are.

# My son's having health problems

*I am concerned about my son. His birth date is 24 April 1966. Since we have had his bedroom extension done, he has had health problems.*

*His headboard is on the east, so when sleeping my son faces west, with his feet facing the TV. A big window is on the north, a small window on the east. Wardrobes on the south wall are aligned with the door. The bathroom is on the west and slightly on the south-west. The wall between the bedroom and the bathroom is west.*

*Please help me to place things in the proper way. Thanking you, Sushi*

Dear Sushi

Based on his date of birth, your son's KUA number is 7, which makes him a west-group person. You say that his health problems started after the extension to his bedroom. It is likely that the renovations inadvertently offended one of the three Flying Star afflictions related to renovations. In addition, you will find that all his windows open in the east direction, and even his sleeping direction (i.e. where his head is pointed when lying down) is an east direction. The one good direction – west – is occupied by the toilet. So the room is all wrong for your son. Best to move him to another room, where all the directions are west rather than east. The west directions are west, south-west, north-west and north-east.

# Can I feng shui a sick room?

*I just heard from a friend that her best friend has liver cancer. Most of the surgical attempts at stopping the cancer have not worked. They tried reiki, with no success. They are moving her to a hospice. Is there anything that can be done to her hospice room that can help at all? Thanks and god bless, Sydney*

Dear Sydney

I hope and pray so. Try letting her sleep with the head pointed to her personal tien yi direction. Since it is the liver that is giving problems, it is a good idea to strengthen the earth element of the home. Place a big cluster of crystals in the south-west of her home. Do not display red flowers in the hospice room; yellow flowers are best. Play some light music and, if possible, ask the patient to chant the mantra of the Medicine Buddha.

This is known to be extremely calming and soothing. It is also excellent for encouraging better health, if the karma of the patient allows it. The mantra of the Medicine Buddha is: tayata om bhaykandze, bhaykandze, maha bhaykandze, ratna samu gate' soha. Try to visualize a Buddha with a body in deep and bright-blue colours as the mantra is chanted.

## I work a lot with computers

*I am a computer graphics designer, so I work with computers nearly 16 hours a day. How can I prevent myself from possible harm from so much exposure to the computer? Regards, Ron*

Dear Ron

Get up and go for a walk every hour or so. This allows you to breathe in some yang chi. Play some music as you work – you can always use a Walkman. The idea is to give your body chi a chance to move and flow.

# Sleepless nights

*I am constantly suffering from insomnia. Can feng shui help? Betty*

Dear Betty

If there is a beam directly above you, move your bed out of the way. Or check whether your bedroom is subject to excessive western sunlight during the afternoons. If so, invest in some heavier curtains. Excessive yang energy often causes sleepless nights.

# Constant health problems

*My wife is seldom free from pain, whether it be migraines, toothache or sinus-related afflictions. Although we have many books on feng shui, we cannot find anything in them to help. Please could you give us any tips you may have. My wife is called Anne, born on 6 April 1954. Thank you, Richard*

Dear Richard

Pain is usually caused by chi being blocked inside. Perhaps you could ask her to do some gentle exercise. Taking up chi kung should help, since this will help her to clear the blocks in her personal flow of chi. There are also special herbs that can be taken to help dissolve these blocks and alleviate her pain. From a feng shui perspective, headaches and health problems relating to pain may be due to an afflicted north-west. Please check the north-west corner of your bedroom. See if there is a bright light there. If so, remove it and the migraines may improve. If there is a window here that gets hit by bright afternoon sunlight, keeping the curtains closed might also help.

## Feng shui for home health

*Please could you help me with regard to taking a home course on feng shui? I have been housebound for about three months and until I have seen a specialist and been diagnosed I cannot proceed with my life as it was. I may not be able to continue in my employment as a laboratory technician and so, thinking positively, I would like to learn more about feng shui. Plus the fact that some of the practices could be beneficial to my general well-being and health.*

*I have tried (unsuccessfully) to find home courses here in England, and it appears an unpopular approach to take a home course with a view to becoming a practitioner. However, I don't have much choice in the matter and would appreciate any advice you can give to help me. Sonnie*

Dear Sonnie

Instead of a home course I would suggest that you get yourself some good books and a computer. Then read the books and surf the Net – a whole new world of feng shui will open up to you. It is a wonderful world, in which you will learn about the powerful invisible and intangible life force called chi. You will learn to balance your personal chi with the chi of the environment.

At the same time, try to get a book that contains the KUA formula and then sleep with your head pointed in the tien yi (or Doctor from Heaven) direction. This might make you feel a lot better physically. Next, get a cluster of crystals and place them in the north-east of your bedroom. This should ignite the search for knowledge strongly in your mind and motivate you in your quest for further information.

# Can dragons hurt us?

*Both my daughter and I were born in the Year of the Dog and we have read somewhere that dogs and dragons are "natural enemies"... This has been rather disturbing and we are wondering if the ceramic dragon that we have placed on the east table of our living room will cause us harm? To make matters worse (we think), we also belong to the east group (based on the KUA formula), so surely putting the dragon there in the east will hurt us? Please let us know what you think. Thank you very much. Pat*

Dear Pat

Yes indeed, dragons and dogs clash rather dramatically, according to Chinese astrology, but the dragon of astrology and the feng shui dragon are quite different. The dragon is the universal celestial symbol that brings good fortune to everyone (even those born in dog years), so I really would not worry. The dragon in the east brings enormous good fortune, and especially good health to the family. Having said this, please note that the Year of the Dragon is not so good a year for dog people.

# Terrible nightmares!

*I have recently moved into a small, one-bedroom home (around 60 years old) with wooden floorboards. The bedroom faces the front of the house near the front door, with the window facing out on to the street. As it is a small room, the only way I can comfortably put my bed is so that my feet are facing towards the window, with a chest at the foot of the bed. There is a mirror facing the bedroom door and a crystal hanging in the window.*

*Since moving into the property I have had terrible nightmares and would like to know how to overcome this. Is there anything I can do to stop the nightmares? Regards, Denby*

Dear Denby

What kind of nightmares? If they are the sort that scare you half to death, perhaps there could be the presence of a lingering entity, which might have to be appeased. One way of coping with this sort of affliction is to do some spiritual space-clearing. Try using a mixture of salt and rice grains. Walk through each of the rooms in a circular clockwise direction sprinkling the mixture; then, as you sprinkle, offer the rice grains to appease and the salt to cleanse. Do this three times round each room. If you know any mantras, chant these as you walk round the rooms... Make sure that the windows and doors are left open as this will allow the chi to flow freely in and out of the room as you do this. Also keep the lights turned on.

The nightmares should stop after this and you should sleep soundly. In the meantime, check that there are no heavy beams or pointed structures above your bed, as these cause your inner chi to be "pressed down".

## Can feng shui help me lose weight?

*I would like to improve my health by losing weight. I've read that you should write on a piece of paper what you want to achieve, place it in a red envelope, then put the envelope in the area you'd like to improve (for me this would be health). Is this true? If it is, would that be all I need to do? If I place it in the health corner, would that be the health corner of the whole house or the health corner of my bedroom or living room? I'm not sure. Thanks for your help and time. Yours, Misty*

Dear Misty

I have to confess I haven't heard of this red envelope trick. I do know that feng shui cannot help much in losing weight. Believe me, I wish I could use feng shui to lose a few pounds! What I do know is that if you want to have good health, you should sleep with your head pointing in the health direction (tien yi), based on the KUA formula. Also, it helps to place longevity symbols around the home, like the god of longevity, bamboo, tortoises, and so forth.

# 5

# Money Matters

## HOW TO KEEPING THE
## CASH FLOWING

Feng shui provides a multitude of cures for cash-flow crises to bring you the prosperity and peace of mind you deserve. First, invest some money to attract money luck. Go shopping for an ornamental "money toad", replica Chinese coins and a money plant. Display wealth gods, money vases and cargo laden sailing ships in the south-east corner of your living room. Tie the coins together with red cord or ribbon and place them in your purse or wallet – and wait for your income luck to jump right in. The effects of bad feng shui can be equally dramatic, thereby draining your resources and leaving you at the mercy of your bank manager. From the dangers of open staircases to waterbeds, missing wealth corners to mirrors, here's my guide to surviving the financial jungle and making money come your way.

*Aunt Agga*

# The miracle "wealth plant"

*I have been told that by placing a particular type of plant in my home, it will encourage financial success and that, if the plant was to perish, I should not be concerned, because it perishes by absorbing all the negative energies. My question is: what type of plant, or plants? I am at a stage where I need all the help I can get. Your reply will be very much appreciated. Best wishes, Heather*

Dear Heather

Gee whizz, I would love to have such a magic plant too! Are you referring to the wealth plant? If so, no, it does not absorb all your negative energies. What it does do is symbolize wealth and attract a great deal of wealth luck into your home. It looks like pieces of oval jade stuck on a stem, and is thus sometimes referred to as the jade plant. It grows freely in California and is easy to find in Europe, but is less common in the Tropics.

# What is wrong with dried flowers?

*(Thank you so much for a wonderful column!) Lillian Too's Little Book of Feng Shui at Work says, "Never use dried plants or arrangements. These emit unlucky energies." This is of great concern to me – my house is filled with dried grasses, lotus pods, papyrus, dried gypsophila, etc. I've kept the thatch and dried-flower garlands that I made for my wedding and have them in my lounge. How can this be unlucky? Please explain further. Thank you so much, Theresa*

Dear Theresa

Only because dried leaves and flowers emit strong yin energy, and this could create an excess that might bring illness and bad luck. In feng shui it is always better to be surrounded by living things rather than dead, even if they are symbolic. That is the reason why Lillian advises against dried flowers.

# Water beds and financial problems

*I am new to the wonders of feng shui. I have started reading your answers to the questions people send you. I did get the message that there should be absolutely no water in the bedroom. As I sleep on a water bed, my question is: do I have to get rid of the bed? I am of the sign of the goat, born on 5 September 1943 at 1.05 a.m. (continental Europe). My financial life is a mess. I earn well, but the more I earn, the more unexpected payments have to be made, and I end up with zero every month. What am I to do? Thank you very much for your advice, and lots of love, Natalie*

Dear Natalie

This will always be the story of your life unless you get rid of your water bed. Sorry, but firstly the water will cause financial loss and, secondly, the water bed means that you sleep on an unstable base every night. Tell me how that can be good feng shui?

# Making wealth adjustments

*I follow your column on-line each month and your advice has improved
my life in many ways. I need your advice, however, on a problem. I have
made several wealth adjustments to my home, which have improved my
income considerably. However, I have not been able to reap the rewards
of this new-found prosperity. Each time I think I am getting ahead,
something happens that causes my money to be spent.*

*For example, car repairs, an outstanding college bill, or the heat in
my home needs fixing, etc. What can I do to remedy this situation? I
have followed your advice religiously, so any suggestions are greatly
appreciated. Thanks, Laurie*

Dear Laurie

Hey, come on, I can teach you feng shui, but I cannot teach you cash
management. Look at it this way: if you had not improved your income
luck, you would be short of money by now. Things like car repairs, air-
conditioning bills and college bills are expenses that are incurred by most
people in your situation. One way of solving your problem would be to read
some more and see how else you can use feng shui. Go deeper to find out
if there may be other things you can do to enhance your luck in other areas.

# Water in the south-east

*In Creating Abundance Lillian Too advises that it is good feng shui to
activate the south-east (wealth sector) with water and green plants. In
The Complete Illustrated Guide to Feng Shui she mentions that it is
extremely bad to have water in the right-hand corner facing the main door.*

*In my shop the south-east corner (wealth sector) happens to be the
right-hand corner from my main door when facing out. I have
activated the water element in this corner with a small water fountain
to concentrate on wealth. Should this be moved? Looking forward to
hearing from you soon, Karla*

Dear Karla

Activating the south-east brings money and income enhancement –
so for your shop it is fine...in fact, it is very good. Only in your home, if there
is water on the right-hand side, is there danger of the man of the house
developing a roving eye. The money will still be good, but togetherness is
affected. In the place of work it does not matter.

# Money is running out of the house!

*My house has a lot of beams on the ceiling. Can you give me a solution for this? Also, our stairs are open (i.e. you can see through from all levels). Can you recommend any solutions? Both my husband and I are working, but we are always just making ends meet. Money seems to be running out. Regards, Anna*

Dear Anna

The beams are not a problem if they form part of the overall pattern and design of the home, but keeping the house brightly lit will help dissolve the harmful energy created by the edges of the beams. What you need to do is cover the "holes" in your staircase. This is what is causing your money to haemorrhage. Use a carpet and some pieces of wood to do this – and please do it soon.

## The Black Hat Sect method

*I just want one thing clarified. As I enter our front door (on the lower-ground level and to be painted red) and stand in the middle of the entrance hall, I face the front door for a compass reading, which states that the front door faces south. I have set all my standards by this.*

*My north-west corner of the house is on a staircase. I have pictures of birds to help lift the chi, and plants at the bottom of both sets of stairs (it is a three-storey mews). The first set of stairs leads straight down to the entrance and faces the front door. One of my pictures on the north wall is a water scene, but painted in autumn colours – not black. The water is of course blue, but a lot of the landscape is in shades of pink. Is this okay?*

*Some practitioners say that the north wall of each room is the wall you face as you enter the room. Which method would you use for a mews house in London? When I feng shui my desk, it is facing south-west. Do I take the reading for the north of my desk as being the centre of my desk as I sit at it, or the literal compass reading of north, which would be to my right? Thank you for clarifying these points. Very sincerely, Anne*

Dear Anne

Firstly, by using the compass reading you are applying the authentic Chinese method of feng shui, which uses only this method for taking directions. Feng shui is all about directions and orientations. None of the authentic feng shui masters of the world use the door to mark out the north and, by extension, all the other directions. That is the Black Hat Sect method, which I do not follow. The picture on your north wall sounds perfectly fine...although of course a spring picture is always to be preferred to an autumn picture. At your desk use a compass to find out your exact sitting direction. Later you will find that all the advanced methods of feng shui make recommendations based entirely on the directions of the compass.

## Which number is better?

*I'm in the process of renting offices for my Internet start-up business. The numbers offered to me are 36 or 37. Kindly advise as to which is the more auspicious, from a feng shui viewpoint. Nishet*

Dear Nishet

During this period of seven, the number 37 is better. Also, since the numbers add up to 10, this makes it better. It also indicates that having a water feature near the entrance would be auspicious.

# Real estate, sitting positions and a suicidal arrowana fish

*I have written several times, with no response from you. I hope you will answer this time. What auspicious symbols should be displayed for someone in the real-estate business? If my sitting position in the office faces my sheng chi direction, but is between two walls where toilets are located, what needs to be corrected? (There is no other way of repositioning it.)*

*Meanwhile a recently purchased arrowana was found dead on the floor and I cannot understand how this fish managed to get out of the tank at such a height. Is this a bad omen? Should a replacement be made or should the idea be abandoned? Teik Ee*

Dear Teik Ee

People in the real-estate business benefit from the placement of crystals in the foyer of their office. It is also extremely beneficial if the doors of the office (back and front) face the earth directions (i.e. south-west or north-east).

There is nothing wrong with your sitting position. The toilets do not harm you unless you share a wall with a toilet.

Finally, your arrowana jumped out of the tank and committed suicide – nothing strange in this. Arrowanas are very strong fish and they can jump to heights many times their own size. The top of the tank must always be kept covered. It is neither a good nor a bad sign, but it does suggest that another kind of fish might suit you better. Although the arrowana is said to be the wealth fish, I have discovered that goldfish are just as good in bringing the money rolling in. In any case, good luck to you.

# Increasing trading profits

*I am a trader (who has lost tons of money) and also a west-group person. What is your best suggestion to improve my stock-trading profits? Thank you very much for reading my e-mail. Johan*

Dear Johan

The best way to increase your trading profits is always to trade while facing your sheng chi direction, or at least one of the west-group directions (which are west, south-west, north-west and north-east). Then it might help if you surround yourself with a couple of wealth symbols, like three old Chinese coins tied with red thread, the three-legged toad or the image of a terrapin (dragon fish). And stick three coins energized with red thread on your telephone, since you will probably be doing much of your trading by telephone.

# Mountains, pigs and dragons

*I read Lillian Too's article on "Increasing wealth in the coming year of the Golden Dragon" in your on-line magazine and thought I would like to ask a question. I read about having a picture of a mountain. I live in the mountains of Colorado and have a beautiful view of the snow-capped mountains from the glass-enclosed room that I use as an office. Inside here I have my computer, my kuan yin, my crystals, waterfall, rocks, plants, mirrors and lace trimmings... I love the feel of my room, perhaps because I have the mountains behind me while I sit at work. My question is: since I have the mountains, do I also need to add a picture of mountains?*

*Additionally, I was born in the Year of the Pig, and while my intuition tells me to decorate this new house in lots of gold, I was told by an astrologer that the Chinese Year of the Dragon would eat my pig funds and that it would not be a good year for me to start a new business. Could you comment on how I could use feng shui and what I can do to make things more in my favour... Jade*

Dear Jade

It sure sounds like you live in a beautiful part of the world. No, with the Rocky Mountains behind you, you do not need any picture of mountains. The real thing is a thousand times better. Just always make sure that the mountain is behind you and never in front of you.

As for what your astrologer told you, well, I don't know about dragons eating up pig funds. From what I know of dragons, this celestial creature brings wealth, but never takes it away. The dragon year is great for everyone except those born in the Year of the Dog, who should lie low. Pig-year people will benefit. It is in the Year of the Snake that pig-year people will have bad luck in, not the Year of the Dragon.

# Unlucky numbers

*I am about to start a small business and have rented an office lot. The thing is, the numbers associated with the office have lots of fours in them. I know the number four sounds like "die" in Chinese. And the office's numbers (i.e. 94-2 and 4/91) sound pretty bad in Cantonese. Does the sound of numbers really have anything to do with feng shui? If so, what can I do to improve (or completely reverse) this bad feng shui, short of moving out? I am quite lost here and would really appreciate your advice. If the answers are in any of your books that I may not have read, please tell me which ones. Thank you very much, J.H.*

Dear J.H.

Yes, many people believe that the number four is very bad luck! In both the Cantonese and Hokkien dialects it means "to die". But according to Chinese numerology, the number four usually means romance luck or literary luck. For some it is also an excellent lucky number, we know many tycoons in Hong Kong for whom the number four has brought good fortune. So I would not worry too much about this number. In feng shui it is the numbers five and two that one should worry about.

# Canal flowing in the wrong direction

*According to Lillian Too's book, the canal that flows in front of our home is moving in the wrong direction. Our home is orientated facing the direction of south-west. The canal water is moving from left to right, and according to her book this is most inauspicious...but what can we do? Here in Amsterdam it is impossible to change the direction of the door or of the canal flow. Have you any suggestions? Since living here, our work has been steadily going downhill... Albert*

Dear Albert

According to the water formula, all houses oriented to the cardinal directions should have water flow moving from left to right, and all houses oriented to secondary directions should have water flowing from right to left. In your case, therefore, the flow is not auspicious and it seems a waste, because a good flow of water brings great good fortune. It is best to block the view of the water altogether, either by planting trees by the edge of the canal or by having curtains. Trees are the best solution, since the wood element will then control the inauspicious water element.

# I've tried everything, but am still poor...help!

*Honestly, I have all of Lillian Too's books and I have done everything – yes, everything – she has suggested and still I am as poor as a church mouse. Please tell me what else I can do? Jerry*

Dear Jerry

Perhaps you might wish to consider putting some ideas into action and working hard to achieve success. Feng shui is certainly not a magical science. What it can do is bring opportunities your way – but whether you become rich or successful depends on how you use these opportunities. We Chinese believe in the trinity of luck, tien it ren – the luck from heaven, the luck from earth and mankind luck. So feng shui is earth luck. But you still need to make your own luck, which you must create for yourself. So do get started!

# Three-legged toads

*I have a question about three-legged toads. Lillian Too recommends that the three-legged toads should be placed under a table or inside a cupboard. But in the illustration the toad is under a sofa. In her latest book she recommended that we place them "waist-high" on a coffee table. Now I am not sure what to do any more. I would really appreciate it if you could clarify this point. Many thanks in advance. Anonymous*

Dear Anonymous

The three-legged toad is just that – a toad that hops all over the place... As long as they are not placed too high up, or directly in front of the door as though about to hop out, it is fine wherever you put them. You should have fun with them... Lillian says to tell you she has nine of them hopping all over her living room.

# 6

# Getting Seriously Rich

## ATTRACTING WEALTH

This chapter is not for the unambitious. Some letters I receive implore me to grant them wealth and possibly fame, or serious riches with a lifestyle to match. I have to point out that I am not a magician but, nevertheless you don't have to be naïve or desperate to strike gold, because just believing in your goal, establishing your inner intent to succeed, is the first step to success. Here, I reveal some of the most potent feng shui symbols of wealth that you can activate at home, from the Chinese gods of wealth to using water, fish and even the octagon shape to magnetize opportunities. Using feng shui for riches means good fortune can find you. And when it does, be sure to create good karma by passing on a little of your luck to others!

*Aunt Agga*

# My burning ambition

*My burning ambition is
to become famous and rich.
So at my office I try to face
my sheng chi direction. My
problem is that, no matter
how hard I try, this is simply
not possible. My question
therefore is: are there any
other changes I can implement
to improve my office luck?
Also, is it possible to change
someone's personality with
feng shui? I hope some
day I can be famous.
What can I do to
achieve this?
Cherie*

Dear Cherie

Well, I must applaud your single-minded determination to become famous and rich. I am sure that your own efforts will see you to the top, but of course feng shui can also give you a helping hand.

There are many things you can do to improve your feng shui luck. To become famous, you should always take care of your south corner. So make sure that it is well lit, and also that it is painted bright red after the year 2001. Keep lights in the south turned on throughout the day and night.

To become rich you should activate the number eight Water Star in the Flying Star chart of your home. Now if you are really determined, you will make every effort to find out how to do this. Here's a clue. Try to get a copy of my book on Flying Star, study it and then see if you can find where the number eight Water Star in your apartment is located. Then (if it is not inside your bedroom) place an aquarium there. This should get the money flowing right in! Then, once you are rich, you can become famous if you use your money wisely to do good for others.

# Is water feng shui the key to wealth?

*I have read somewhere that wealth is synonymous with water and that to really get rich with feng shui it is necessary to have big auspicious water, such as rivers and waterfalls. My question is: does that mean people who live in cities cannot get seriously rich? Does it mean that where this type of natural water is missing, or difficult to incorporate into one's feng shui, such places cannot bring wealth? Iskandar*

Dear Iskandar

Perhaps I should answer your questions one at a time. Yes, to the Chinese and in feng shui lore, water is strongly associated with wealth, and good water features correctly placed in and around the home always bring wealth. How much wealth it brings depends on other factors as well – for example, your quota of what we term "heaven luck" or, as the Buddhists prefer to call it, your "karma". So yes, water is very important in creating good wealth feng shui.

However, this does not mean that those living in cities cannot benefit from water. Indeed, if you think about it, almost all the great cities of the world grew up around rivers – all the most successful urban centres were built around one big river. London, New York, most of the great cities of Europe, Asia and Australia stand on rivers or waterways – so it doesn't mean that city people are not able to get rich. In any case, feng shui offers countless different ways of energizing water, and of using different manifestations of water. Thus, if you live in the city, you can always put up a painting of a river scene on the correct wall of your living room – and it will attract wealth for you! So there's no need to lose heart just because you live in a city.

# A case of too many wealth energizers

*I have followed the advice of two feng shui masters and have built a beautiful aquarium in my office. They explained that, since I am a wood person, water is excellent for me. I have filled these aquariums with 108 goldfish, because I was told that this was a magical number. My problem is that my goldfish keep dying, and to date I have lost count of the number of dead fish. The feng shui man has told me not to worry, since the goldfish have supposedly taken away my bad luck by dying. But it has been a depressing exercise and, far from bringing me good luck (or taking away my bad luck), I seem to be suffering more loss than gain. My business has gone downhill since installing the aquarium and I am seriously thinking of doing away with it altogether. My letter to you is in the hope that I may get a solution to my problem. John*

Dear John

Wow! How big is your aquarium, may I ask? 108 goldfish is a lot and, magic number or not, this seems like a ridiculous number of fish. So I am not surprised that they keep dying. With so many fish in your tank there is sure to be a high rate of death. Lillian Too advises having only nine goldfish. If one or two die, it is perfectly fine to replace them; and yes, according to feng shui, the fish have helped you avoid some loss. But when fish die due to overcrowding, then excessive yin energy has been created... So my worry for you is that your tank may be too large and that you definitely have too many fish. Wealth energizers should not be overdone. Too much water can drown you!

So take your fish back to the shop, change the water, make sure the filter is working efficiently and then restock with just nine goldfish. And make certain that the tank has been placed in front of you and not behind you. It is also better to have water in the north or east wall.

## My sailing ship is not working

*I have read that if I put a sailing ship in my office, my sales will increase many times over. Well, that is exactly what I did. I bought a small sailing ship and, although it has been three months since I did that, nothing has happened. My sales performance continues to be average and my income has not increased. Did I do something wrong? Esther*

Dear Esther

A couple of fine points here that it might be useful for you to check. Firstly, did you put some "pretend" gold on the ship? Secondly, did you make sure that the ship is sailing in and not out? And thirdly, what kind of ship is it? The best types of ship to use are the sailing junks used by old Chinese merchants at the start of the nineteenth century, because these ships brought much gold and wealth each time they came into harbour. Also, note that merchant sailing ships are different from the sports variety. Plus, make sure that there are no cannons on your ship!

# ...And my sailing ship is magical – thank you

*I have to write and tell you that since placing a sailing ship in the foyer of our office, we have been inundated with orders and now there is simply too much business and we cannot cope. I have ordered six more of these ships from Vietnam and would like to ask if it is okay for me to put more than one ship in one office? Also, if I give the ships away as gifts, does this mean I am giving away my wealth? Please advise, and many thanks to you again, Meera*

Dear Meera

Obviously you have discovered a very well-kept secret – these wonderful model sailing ships from Vietnam are simply perfect. They are cheap and very well done. And they are exactly right for feng shui purposes. I take it you have also filled your ship with "gold ingots" – the fake variety will do just as well. To answer your questions: it is perfectly fine to put more than one ship in each office. This turns your office into a teeming and bustling harbour. Many ships signify that the winds and the waters are bringing wealth to you! Also, each ship represents one source of income and many ships represent many sources of income. And yes, give them away as gifts. The best gift is to give away something you value – it shows a real generosity of heart and is good for your feng shui. Feng shui never likes a vacuum, so the moment you give anything away, something similar or better comes right back...

# Is our waterfall auspicious?

*We have a waterfall fountain in the south-east corner of our garden in full view of the main door which faces south, with the flow of water in a semi-circle towards the house (the shape of a kidney, with the concavity towards the house's main door). Is the feng shui auspicious? We have a blue gate and blue wall around the waterfall. Is this acceptable? Please let us know what colour is auspicious – white or pink or light brown – and the roof the normal red roof-tile colour? By the way, my KUA number is 7. Please advise before I start on the job. Thanks, Dr. Muthu*

Dear Dr. Muthu

A waterfall like you describe in the south-east is excellent, especially since it is also on the left-hand side of the main door. As for the colour of the tiles, blue or white is fine. Pink is not so harmonious. The red roof is also good. The only thing I want to caution you about is that the size of the waterfall must not overwhelm the house, and this is of course a matter of judgement. Also, make certain that there is some land between where the water collects and your main door. When water is too near the house itself, it tends to represent financial danger, which means a danger of loss of money.

## Water-wall in the living room

*We have a most beautiful wall in my living room, which has water sort of flowing down the wall. It does not look like a waterfall. Instead, it resembles just a sheet of water, which looks very nice with plants and lights. We have had this for a year now and so far it has been neither good nor bad in terms of luck. Last week someone came and told us that the wall, being a west wall, is not good.*

*Can you please advise us what to do, as we really like our water-wall... but of course we also want good luck. My friend has indicated that the wall will eventually cause severe harm to our children. Is this possible?*
*Jacek*

Dear Jacek

You see, water in the west exhausts the metal element of the west. Since the west is an indicator of children's well-being, especially for those who have reached the age of young adults, having the entire west wall flowing with water is indeed a big risk to take. Naturally my statement must be read within a feng shui perspective. Your friend is therefore right in alerting you to the danger. If you do not want to remove the wall, here are a couple of things you can do to "weaken" the effect of the water.

Firstly, place plenty of plants here. This represents the wood element which weakens the water. Wood is also under the control of metal. Secondly, keep the place well-lit, so that water becomes a source of power rather than a source of heartache. These two solutions should help to keep your water-wall under control.

# Auspicious Flying Star

*My mother brought a feng shui consultant to the house the other day and he told us to place a water fountain in the north corner of our house. According to him, our Flying Stars in the north indicate great wealth and by making a water fountain here, we will be activating the wealth chi. The north happens to be at the back of the house and I read somewhere that water behind is not good, as it represents missed opportunities. Please advise on this contradiction. Mariam*

Dear Mariam

Yes, it is correct that if the Flying Water Star is auspicious in any sector, then activating that sector with water will bring enormous wealth luck and make your family seriously rich. So if it has been diagnosed that the north is where you need to put the water feature, then I would support the recommendation, even though the north is behind your house. The way to overcome this is to open a door here – have your back door here and keep it open. Or, if this is difficult, at least have a window so that the auspicious energized chi can fly in. And another thing: a waterfall flowing towards your home is better than a fountain.

# Is a swimming pool at the back okay?

*We have a small swimming pool at the back of our house. This is the back-garden area, where we spend most of our time. The pool is rectangular in shape and is located south of the house. It cannot be seen from the back door, as it is very nicely hidden away and surrounded by tall trees. We read that the south conflicts with water, but since we live in South Africa which is in the southern hemisphere, does this mean that our swimming pool is like being in the north and will thus bring lots of money? Sincerely, Draymond*

Dear Draymond

Well, firstly, the directions of the compass do not change, irrespective of whether you are in the northern or southern hemisphere. And to answer your question: yes, water does clash with the fire of the south; but in your case, with the pool hidden away surrounded by trees, it signifies hidden wealth. Having the pool at the back of the house is fine if your family spends time there. But if the back is left quiet most of the time, then excessive yin energy could build up causing some bad effects. I am generally wary of swimming pools, because of the danger of their being too overpowering for the home. While water brings great good-wealth luck, it can also cause severe financial problems leading to bankruptcy, when pools are placed wrongly or if they are too big.

## Feng shui gifts

*I would like to know if it is all right to buy items such as the three-legged frog, coins and crystals for other people, or should they purchase these items themselves? Anonymous*

Dear Anonymous

These items make wonderful and delightful gifts, as they represent such good sentiments. You are most kind to wish others great abundance and prosperity. In fact whenever you send someone a gift that is accompanied by goodwill sentiments, you are sharing your own positive and auspicious chi . This instantly creates a vacuum for yet more positive chi to come to you. This is part of inner feng shui practice. To give is one of the best ways of enhancing your own store of good fortune chi, and the better your gift, the higher will be the quality of chi that you attract.

## Mad about arrowanas

*Lillian Too makes frequent references to the arrowana, and I just want to say that we have some prize specimens of this fish – our golden arrowana is worth several thousand dollars, but we have been keeping these graceful fish for many years now and they have yet to bring us great wealth... Please can you advise where is the best place to keep them, how many we should keep and whether there is any difference in the type of arrowana to keep. Mei Jen*

Dear Mei Jen

The arrowana is indeed the "feng shui fish" and many business tycoons all over Asia keep at least one arrowana in their homes. The correct variety is, surprisingly, the least expensive of the species. This is the silver-coloured variety with a pink tinge to the tail. The tail itself tapers to one end-fin, while the expensive variety ends in a double fin. This is because the correct silver/pink arrowana is shaped like a sword and this is said to "kill off" all bad luck. It is strongly believed that, if placed correctly (i.e. in the north, east or south-east corners of the home), they bring success and great money luck . Usually the time taken is less than a year, which also coincides with them growing to a length of about 30cm. (12in.). It is also best to keep a single arrowana, but if you like to keep more than one, then five would be a good number.

## Which "god of wealth" should we keep?

*I did not realize there were so many different gods of wealth until I visited Hong Kong recently. Since becoming interested in feng shui and reading about the Chinese god of wealth in Lillian Too's book, I have been wanting to present my husband with a god of wealth – something he sorely needs. But with so many to choose from, how do I know which one to get? And where do we place it to obtain the maximum benefits? Genevieve*

Dear Genevieve

If your husband is in business or in a high-flying corporate career, then the best god of wealth to get is Kuan Kong, who is also the god of war. This deity is believed to afford protection from people who have bad intentions, as well as bring money luck. He is usually shown with a fierce countenance and holding big weapons. Those who want good fortune in money luck for the whole family might want to get Tsai Shen Yeh – the god of wealth that sits on a tiger. Actually, it does not matter which one you get. But do display it in a place of prominence and respect (e.g. not on a low coffee table).

## Does the octagonal shape symbolize luck?

*A very close and wealthy friend of mine built his own home. The design that permeates most of the living space – both inset ceilings and floor design – is octagonal. I asked about this and he said that the octagon is the symbol for luck in Chinese. Any truth to this? Thank you, Anonymous*

Dear Anonymous

To the Chinese, the octagonal shape is the shape of the Pa Kua. And yes, this is considered a lucky shape. However, do not confuse things by thinking that hanging the Pa Kua is therefore also lucky. Most Pa Kuas that are sold in Chinese shops (for hanging) include the eight trigrams and these are usually arranged according to the Earlier Heaven arrangement. These Pa Kuas are sold for combating poison arrows and bad energy. For example, if you have a tall tree opposite your front door, you can hang a Pa Kua on your front door to reflect back the shar chi that it is sending you. But don't hang such Pa Kuas inside the home. This will be harmful to you and to everyone else who lives in the house.

# 7

# How To Attract Love

## HOW TO FIND THE RIGHT PARTNER

Attracting a soulmate can't always be left to fate. Why wait? Decide that you want to find love with feng shui and you'll meet that special person. Using this ancient practice to attract love is, however, intensely powerful, bringing romantic opportunities with long-term potential - so be sure that you're ready for a relationship before you begin. Simply activate your love corner – this is the south-west of your home. Place a red lamp or lantern there to literally light up your love life; add two mandarin ducks, or display the Chinese double-happiness symbol. And to really make love energy soar, wear my stunning double-happiness jewellery. Remember, the cycle of chi energy is 28 days – so within one month you'll see your love dreams materialize. Enjoy!

*Aunt Agga*

# Badly wanting a boyfriend

*My name is Eva. I was born on 2 August 1972 in Poland. I came to the USA six years ago. I've got some of Lillian Too's books which I like very much. The reason I am writing is that I need your advice. I think that I have bad luck because of the things that have happened to me over these six years. I can take a lot, but there is one thing that has made me sad all the time – romance. I'm 27 years old and I have never had a boyfriend. I'm not ugly; I'm 1.57m.(5ft. 6in.) tall, 54kg. (120lb.), with black hair, and people would say that I'm beautiful, but my love life is nonexistant. I would like to meet someone who will love me.*

*Aunt Agga, please help me. In September last year I bought eight Chinese peonies (red) and placed them in a metal vase in the west corner of my living room. I also got mandarin ducks (two) and placed them in the south-west of my bedroom. I got fish, crystals, windchimes, mountain pictures, etc., but it seems that nothing will work. What else can I do? It may seem funny that a boyfriend is so important to me, but most of my friends are married, have families here, and boyfriends and girlfriends. If you can help me I would be so grateful. Eva*

Dear Eva

Do you live alone? Are you sleeping with your head pointing in your love direction? Have you properly energized the south-west of your bedroom? What do you do? Are you shy?

From a feng shui viewpoint, it is not that difficult to get a boyfriend. But finding a good man who will cherish and love you – that is not so easy. From your letter I think you are trying too many things, without taking care to do them properly. Start again, take down all the objects you mentioned above and then do the following. Do not do more than this – just the three things I am recommending are sufficient.

1. Sleep with your head pointing in your nien yen direction, which in your case (based on your date of birth) is west. Please use a good compass to find the direction correctly. If you can also use a west room, this is even better.

2. Place a small red light in the south-west of your bedroom and keep this light on until love comes into your life.

3. Invest in a double-happiness ring made of gold and set with diamonds and wear it all the time. It works extremely quickly.

I hope that this helps you find happiness with a good man.

# Personal life non-existent

*Although I am a person who is very content with life, my personal life is non-existent. My bedroom happens to be in the love/relationship area of my apartment. My wall-to-wall rug is green, so it was recommended that I paint my walls a pale pink, which I have done. I've also burned a pair of candles every night and have placed chimes by the windows. What else can I do to improve this area of my life? Thanks, Joanne*

Dear Joanne

Well, first get rid of the candles and the chimes. Next, replace them with the double-happiness sign and with some pure quartz crystals. A pair of lovebirds also won't hurt. An earth-coloured carpet is required to replace your green carpet. This is because, to activate relationship opportunities, you must energize the earth element. A green carpet signifies wood which destroys earth. Another thing is to change your attitude. You must have a reasonably sound determination to enter into a love relationship for it to happen. You cannot be half-hearted about these things!

# An "unmatched" pair of mandarin ducks

*I have been trying to arrange my bedroom to ensure the best chi and energy to stimulate an on/off relationship, hopefully leading to a commitment. As such, I bought a pair of ceramic ducks, one of which broke before I could get home with it. Unfortunately, I dropped the package it was in. Although I was able to mend it, I replaced it with a "wooden" duck and now have the two in the south-west corner of my room. Is it advisable to pair these together, as they're not a "matched" pair?*

*Also, can you give me some guidelines as to how soon one begins to experience movement or change, upon the proper placement*

*and arrangement of things? Thanks very much for your help. I
look forward to your response. Anonymous*

Dear Anonymous

I sure hope the ducks are a male and a female. Please check. You
might also like to use crystals in the south-west, with a light shining at
them for further romance luck. This will activate the earth energy of that
corner. To answer your second question, usually feng shui works pretty
fast – sometimes even immediately, but usually inside of a month. If it
does not work, then you might be doing something wrong or there could
be another affliction that you may not be aware of (like, for instance, the
Flying Stars not being conducive to a relationship leading to what we call
a "hei see" or happiness occasion – this is a euphemism for a wedding).

## Dismal personal relationships

*All my personal relationships have been very dismal in the past few
years. The house I live in at the moment has an east-facing front door
and a north-facing back (which is the one I use the most), but from the
front door in the far right corner, which I believe is my relationship
corner, are the laundry and toilet. I can't stop using the toilet, but I do
keep the lid down and the door closed as often as possible. What can I
do to improve my situation? My bedroom is in the south-west corner of
the house, and in the relationship corner I have a red-and-white
candle that I burn often. Looking forward to a bright future, Meredith*

Dear Meredith

Do not worry overly much about the toilet. Yes, it does pour cold
water over your love life, but you can activate what we in feng shui call
the "small chi" (as opposed to the "big chi"). This means activating the
relationship corner in your bedroom, instead of in the whole house.
Taking one room to "do" the feng shui is usually just as effective. So
energize your love corner of the bedroom with lights and crystals
and the double-happiness sign. I would avoid using candles if I were
you, as naked flames can be rather dangerous. Lights will do just as well
– especially red lights. But remember never to overdo things. When you
create unbalanced chi by overdoing your feng shui, the result can be
just as bad as having bad feng shui.

## No romance corner to energize

*I do not have a south-west corner in my living room; it is a doorway that leads into the hall for the bedrooms and the bathroom. The south-west corner of my bedroom is the closet. What should I do? Anonymous*

Dear Anonymous

In cases like yours I would advise that you calculate your KUA number based on your date of birth and from there check what your personal love direction is. In feng shui it is called your "nien yen" direction. Please consult any of Lillian's books for this formula. Once you know your love direction, sleep with your head pointing in that direction and sit facing that direction. This will activate good luck in the marriage/family areas of your life.

## Peony painting

*I have hung a large painting of peonies in the east section of the living room. Will it activate good luck and romance for us singles? Regards, Margaret*

Dear Margaret

Indeed yes, it will. The peony is an extremely good symbol to attract marriage luck for the unmarried daughters of the family. At the same time, these peonies will also ensure conjugal bliss when marriage does take place.

## How do you win back love?

*Recently I had a big fight with my boyfriend and we split up. We have spilt up and got back together so many times in the past. However, this time he seems more serious about it. I have tried to talk to him and make advances, but he is not interested. I still love him a lot and know that deep down he loves me too. Anonymous*

Dear Anonymous

Oh dear, it seems like you are basically not compatible, or maybe something is wrong with your Flying Stars, thereby causing you to fight. Okay, to get him back this time, get a big jar of water and place it in the south-west for a while (i.e. until you two are back together again), then remove the still water. But if you are both fundamentally incompatible, perhaps you should split and find someone else? You cannot be using feng shui to patch up quarrels all the time, you know. There will come a time when it simply will not work any more. So think through this one carefully. Besides, consider if this is what you want in a relationship – all this kiss and make up could become a little tedious, don't you think? How much better it is to be cherished, and to cherish someone, so that the urge to fight dissipates... That is what good feng shui brings.

## Wedding plans

*I am planning a wedding at my home, to take place soon. Can you give me some tips on things to do that will strengthen the union and give the guests good luck? Anonymous*

Dear Anonymous

Feng shui for wedding-day decorations involves the use of the auspicious red colour. Use the double-happiness sign and also red lanterns in the home to stimulate the yang energy. And to ensure that the match will lead to lots of bright happy children, look for a virgin child born in the year of the dragon and get him/her to roll across the conjugal bed. There are many different rituals to ensure that the couple stay committed to each other and the families get on well with each other, but these could well fill a book. May I instead recommend you to look for Lillian's book on Chinese symbols of good fortune.

## What book to buy?

*I would like to know which book you would recommend me to buy: I would like help in improving wealth and romance happiness. Thank you, Anonymous*

Dear Anonymous

Lillian's latest book is *Easy-to-use Feng Shui: 168 Ways to Happiness,* which offers all the different feng shui methods to enhance your love life and all your relationships. For wealth she always recommends that attention is given to water feng shui. So I would say her book on gardens would be good for this, because it does contain the water formula.

# Toilet in the south-west

*I am a single male with a KUA number of 8 and I live in a two-bedroom government flat in Singapore. It is unfortunate that the toilet of the master bedroom is located in the south-west direction. Also, my bedroom door is aligned in the same row with the master-bedroom door and the toilet door. And I understand that the south-west corner is also the marriage corner. As you can probably appreciate, living in a government flat makes relocating the toilet an impossible task, so I can only work things round it, and would therefore appreciate any advice you could give.*

*My question is: what should I do to the toilet? Beside not using it and having its door and bowl cover closed at all times? Is it appropriate to hang a windchime in there? And can I activate "marriage chi" using the south-west corner of my bedroom instead of the south-west corner of the flat, which unfortunately is where the toilet is?*

*Lastly, are there any restrictions on the number of windchimes that one can hang around the house, as I intend to hang one in my bedroom and another in the toilet (if appropriate).*

*Appreciate your time and attention. Look forward to your reply and advice. Regards, Ivan*

Dear Ivan

Firstly, if you cannot activate the south-west corner of your bedroom, then place all the love energizers in the south-west of your living room, and then spend lots of time there. Next, for the three doors in a row, hang a windchime above the second door. There is no limit to the number of windchimes you can hang in the house, but never hang a windchime in the south-west, because this will exhaust the energies of the south-west, causing hurt to your chances of getting auspicious marriage luck.

## Main entrance

*My main entrance door happens to be located in the south-west corner of the living room, and the door is facing west. I wonder how I should activate this corner? Kindly advise. Thank you, Joanna*

Dear Joanna

With windchimes, because you are facing west.

# Help – my bathroom is in my love corner!

*Hello, my name is Mariana and I am writing from Lima, Peru. My main concern about feng shui is that in my bedroom I have my bathroom, and it coincides with my love corner. What should I do to activate it? Shoud I first activate the romance corner in my bedroom and then activate it in the bathroom? Please help me as soon as possible because I am desperate. Right now I don't have a boyfriend, or even a close male friend. Help! Sincerely, Mariana*

Dear Mariana

Maybe that's your problem – you are simply too desperate. You need to learn to play it cool and the guys might not feel so threatened. You know, guys really fear a predatory female, so my advice is to go slow. As for your feng shui, you can energize your bedroom, but don't energize the bathroom. Now, if you really do want a boyfirend or lover, invest in a double-happiness ring or a pair of gold and diamond double-happiness earrings, and watch this feng shui jewellery work some nice magic for you. If you cannot afford jewellery, then make your own double-happiness sign and hang it on your bedroom wall behind the bed.

## Too many fish in the sea...

*I was born on 27 November 1965, in Houston, Texas. I am at a point in my life where I have to decide between two men. This is a crucial time for me and I could use any suggestions or advice that you might offer. Thank you in advance, Kimberley*

Dear Kimberley

You can use the KUA formula to choose between them. Usually the man who has the same KUA group (east or west) would be more compatible in terms of it being a more pleasant relationship. It is also easier to feng shui the house of a couple with KUA numbers that are complementary rather than opposing.

## West-group person living in an east house

*H-E-E-E-LP! I'm stuck in the east and I can't get out (smile). Seriously, I recently learned about feng shui and have found to my great dismay that I am a west person (chien) living in an east house (k'an). My personal KUA number is 6, I was born on 4 September 1946, and my house was built in 1917.*

*I read somewhere that to attract a love relationship I should place my bed facing (or pointing) towards the south-west and sleep facing that direction as well. (I have been single for 10 years and have been living in this house for five years.) This does not seem like a good idea to me, because the south-west direction in my house is the death section. Can you help? Thanks, Sharon*

Dear Sharon

Why do you say the south-west is your death direction? If you belong to the KUA of 6, then the south-west is very good for you. However, there seems to be a mistake in your implementation of your directions. Please sleep with your head pointing to the south-west, not your head facing this direction. In any case, if you want to use feng shui to bring you a good relationship, may I suggest that you hang a large picture of the double-happiness symbol in the south-west of your bedroom? It works every time, and is especially good for those with KUA number 6 which as you know means "luck from heaven".

# Hoping for luck in love

*I am 30 years old, divorced, with one child aged seven. I have never had any romantic luck and I am hoping to change this. I have placed a heart-shaped crystal and a hugging couple in the south-west corner of my bedroom. In the north-west corner (my auspicious nien yen direction) of my living room I have placed a pair of mandarin ducks. Is there anything else that I can do? Look forward to hearing from you. Many thanks, Katherine*

Dear Katherine

You can also light up the south-west with a bright light shining at a cluster of crystals, and you can wear the feng shui double-happiness ring or earrings. Most importantly, sleep with your head pointing in your nien yen direction (i.e. to the north-west). You will have even better romance luck if your bedroom is located in the north-west of your home.

# A good match

*My boyfriend is of the metal element and I am of the water element. Are we suitable for each other? Thanks, Sharon*

Dear Sharon

Hey, that's brilliant. Metal produces water. From the element theory alone, it looks as though he will be the one feeding and nurturing you. But what's wrong with that!

# 8

# We Are Not Compatible... Are We?

## IMPROVING RELATIONSHIPS

Is your husband or wife a west-group person, while you're east group? Or you've just discovered that your animal signs clash, and so do your elements and KUA numbers? Believe it or not, you can work it out. Armed with a basic knowledge of lunar astrology, you can neutralize those relationship irritants, boosting your relationship to happy tolerance and even occasional brilliance. Whether you're negotiating with in-laws or checking out the potential of someone you're falling in love with, here's how to begin: look up the animal signs, KUA numbers and elements for you and your partner or relative in the following pages, then read on to discover how to give your household the best chance of happiness. All you need is a little of the Chinese attitude to life and living.

*Aunt Agga*

# Can my husband and I live in the same house?

*According to Lillian Too's KUA formula, my husband and I belong to different groups. My KUA number is 3 and I am an east-group person, but my husband's KUA number is 6, making him a west-group person. Does this mean we cannot live in the same house?*

*At the moment the front door of our house is facing the east direction. We are sleeping in a room that is positioned just above the front door. Please advise us on what we should do. My husband is in the insurance business and I am a housewife. We are not getting along too well and his agency is not doing well. We are also trying to have children, with little success.*

*Each time I ask my husband for money to take care of the household expenses, he appears reluctant and is always finding fault with me. In the evenings when he is back home he ignores me. I am feeling very miserable indeed. If it was not for some financial help from my father, our marriage would have been on the rocks long ago. I don't even know if I want to continue in this marriage, but because we are Indian, divorce is out of the question. Please help us. Mona*

Dear Mona

Oh dear, both the door direction and the bedroom are good for you, but exceedingly bad for your husband. It is possible he may be having problems that you are not aware of, which probably explains his attitude towards you. Perhaps if you improved his feng shui, other things might well improve.

Firstly, find another door that faces one of the west-group directions. Although it will be inauspicious for you, it will help your husband in his work. Next, look for another room in your house which is more suitable for him, and if possible let him sleep with his head pointing in his nien yen or third-best direction. This direction will promote greater harmony between the two of you. Finally, invest in two rice cookers – one for him and one for you. Make sure the two cookers have their plugs facing in different directions – one that is good for you and the other good for him. Many couples can live amicably despite being from different groups.

# I'm in love – but our animal signs are not compatible

*I have fallen madly in love with the girl of my dreams. She is everything I want and admire in the opposite sex, and she loves me in return. Our families are good friends and we have known each other since we were kids, but it is only in recent months that we have discovered that we are true kindred spirits. She likes everything that I like, and we enjoy the same taste in books, films and friends. I feel sure that we will have a future together.*

*Unfortunately I am a snake and she is a pig, according to the Chinese astrology system. According to the elements of the animals, we are fire and water and so we are bad for each other. Fortunately, according to the element of the year of our birth, I belong to the earth element while she belongs to the metal element, which means that I am supposed to be good for her. Will this be okay? Does this mean we are compatible, despite the animal incompatibility? I would like to marry her... Jimmy*

Dear Jimmy

The astrological mismatches are merely superficial indications of compatibility, and I would not worry about it too much, especially since your year elements are most harmonious. Based on your letter, I have calculated that you are an east-group person with a KUA number of 1, while your girlfriend has a KUA of 4 and also belongs to the east group. This indicates that, according to the Eight Mansions KUA formula, you are indeed kindred spirits, so you are most compatible. But don't you think you are both a little young to be making these heavy commitment decisions? From what little information you have given me, it seems that you are 22 and she is only 16 – barely out of school.

# A universal problem

*My husband's KUA number is 7 and my KUA number is 3. Our toilet and oven are located in the south-east of our house. South-east is the lui sha sector of my husband, but it is my nien yen sector. Please advise me what to do. Thank you, Mai Ling*

Dear Mai Ling

Well, you are east group and your husband is west group, just like my husband and me and a great many other couples. The answer to this universal dilemma is to follow the husband's direction when it comes to the main-door direction and sleeping position. For everything else use the individual auspicious direction of each person. In your case, Mai Ling, to compensate for the toilet and oven afflicting your relationship sectors (nien yen), make sure that you have a separate rice cooker that cooks your rice. Then place the cooker so that the electricity is coming into it from your nien yen direction (i.e. from the south-east).

# I'm in love with a married man

*I am embarrassed to write to you with my problem. I have been going out with a married man now for two years and I am beginning to feel more and more that he will never leave his wife. Based on all your books and all the different systems of calculation, he is perfectly suited for me. I have also done everything exactly according to your advice – peonies, mandarin ducks, crystals, and so on... Still he does not wish to leave his wife. He does not love her and he has told me many times that he finds her unattractive. They have not been sleeping together now for a whole year. What can I do? I love him so much. Please don't ask me to leave him, because I simply cannot... Juanita*

Poor foolish Juanita

He will never leave his wife! And you are a fool if you continue to hope that he will. I am sorry, but I really do not condone stealing someone else's husband. I know you love him, but love is no excuse for your behaviour. I don't want to sound unsympathetic, but what if the roles were reversed and you were the long-suffering wife having to put up with an unfaithful husband? No wonder your love energizers do not work. The man you want is not free. And unless, and until, you start finding someone else who is free, your feng shui energizers will continue to be unsuccessful.

# Getting on with mother

*All my life I have had differences with my mother, not only because we have different KUA groups (she is east group and I am west), but also because our animal signs are conflicting (she is a dog and I am a dragon). I would like to get along with her. Can I use feng shui, and if so, how? I am still living with my parents. Agnes*

Dear Agnes

Both of you tapping into your respective good directions and both of you energizing your relationship luck, by strengthening the south-west corners of your bedrooms, will help to improve things between you enormously. The south-west is also the trigram of the matriarch, so strengthening the south-west is an excellent cure for your problem.

# Sibling incompatibility

*I have lived with my widowed sister for three years now and am wondering if feng shui compatibility applies to my situation. I am a 48-year-old spinster and my sister is 55 years old.*

*We used to get on quite well in the old days, but now we are finding it difficult to live in the same house together. The strain between us is forcing me to re-examine whether it might not be better for me to move out altogether. I am writing to you to ask if feng shui can help us live together in a more friendly manner? Betsy*

Dear Betsy

Well, there is no harm in giving it a try. Usually disharmony in a household is due either to conflicting KUA numbers or to afflicted Flying Stars. Here are three suggestions that you might like try to see if things improve for both of you. As it is difficult to give you a Flying Star recommendation in a couple of sentences, I would suggest that you place a six-rod windchime near the front door. This should overcome afflicted Flying Stars (if any) and will not harm good stars located there. Secondly, try changing rooms – this might overcome any problems of chi incompatibility. And thirdly, place an urn of still water at the back of the house. This should absorb any "fighting" energy that might be causing disharmony vibes in the household.

If the situation does not improve after a month, move the water to the front and the windchime to the back. If things still do not improve, perhaps you might want to consider moving into your own place.

# Choosing the right year

*Is there a right year and a wrong year to undertake feng shui changes to correct the incompatibility between couples? Thank you for answering, Harry*

Dear Harry

There is a right and a wrong year for any kind of renovation work. This depends on which part of the house you need to work on and forms part of the Flying Star afflictions. This is something that everyone should investigate properly before undertaking renovation work of any kind.

# Fighting with my wife a lot

*I recently got in touch with feng shui, but I do not seem to be able to do it right, as I have trouble in my marriage – in that we do not see eye to eye and we have been fighting a lot lately. My wife's name is Lauren; her birth date is 30 August 1958 and she was born between 18.00 and 20.00.*

*My birth date is 16 September 1973. I was also born between 18.00 and 20.00. I would very much appreciate it if you could assist me in this matter, as I am desperate for help. Azmi*

Dear Azmi

Well, the first thing to check is your KUA number compatibility. Your KUA number is 9, which makes you an east-group person. Lauren's KUA number is also 9, and this tells me that you are both compatible, so it is easy to do feng shui that is equally good for both of you. If you are arguing it is definitely due to the quarrelsome Flying stars. So I suggest that you use a big jar filled with still water placed near the entrance of your house. This will symbolically capture the fighting stars.

# Husband and wife with clashing KUAs

*I am about to move into my new house somewhere around the end of December/early January. The house is a double-storey link house with its main door facing south, which according to Lillian Too's is my second best direction. The house number is four.*

*According to Lillian's book, I'm (date of birth: 7 October 1960, KUA 4, male) an east person, and my wife (date of birth: 1 October 1965, KUA 7, female) is a west person, which means that we are of different groups. Oh yes! My son (date of birth: 31 August 1997, KUA 3, male) is also an east person.*

*What I find hard to understand is the inside of the house being favourable to the wife and the outside of the house being so for the husband. My wife is a housewife and I'm the sole breadwinner. If the* inside of house is favourable to my wife, it may be destructive to me. And since I have to bring home the earnings to feed my family, shouldn't it be favourable to me? How can a balance be achieved between the differing KUA of spouses without losing out on prosperity and relationships?

I hope you can enlighten me further on how we might improve the feng shui of our new house. Anonymous

Dear Confused Husband

How can the inside of the house be bad for you? Seems to me that the house is most suitable for the husband (both inside and outside), since it faces south and sits north – both of which directions are good for you. The KUA formula is only one formula. There are other formulas and methods that can be used to supplement the KUA formula. That is how to go about maximizing or optimizing your feng shui, even though you belong to different groups with different KUA numbers.

## ...And more clashing KUA numbers

My partner and I would like to buy an apartment together, but our KUA numbers for detailed lucky and unlucky directions are totally different. His is 3 (east group) and mine is 6 (west group), so we do not know what would be the best direction for our main door to face when we select our new home. Please help me regarding the above-mentioned matter, because I'm very confused. Justine

Dear Justine

Many people have this problem. In the old days the Chinese solved this problem by completely ignoring the wife's direction. Feng shui solutions in the modern day suggest a compromise, and so do I. Let the front door face an east direction, east or south-east. This will automatically make the house into a west house, so that it's good for him and for you at the same time. The direction is good for him, but the location is good for you. This is a fine point of feng shui. Why? Because according to the old texts, whenever a house faces a direction it is said to be sitting in the opposite direction. So a house that faces east is said to be sitting west. And a house that faces south-east will be sitting north-west. So this would be one solution. Another solution is to find a house that faces a west direction and thus sits in an east direction.

# Our KUA numbers match,
# but we're opposites

*I have read somewhere that failed marriages and relationships can be due to non-matching Kua numbers and elements. My partner and I have the same KUA number (8) and were born under the same element (wood). Is that a good thing? However, according to Chinese astrology, a tiger and a snake (which is our combination) make a bad match. Would you advise me on all this? Jay*

Dear Jay

Yes, those with the same KUA numbers and year elements do tend to be kindred souls. Usually the number would override any mismatch of animal years, since the animal is only the year earthly branch in Chinese astrology. So in your case you are fine.

Having said that, I must add that many factors go into the quality of a relationship. Astrological indications only give you one-third of the equation. Your feng shui offers the second third and, of course, the remaining third depends on how you both work at making the relationship a fulfilling and happy one.

# Can our zodiac energizers be harmful?

*Is there any danger of the placement of symbols of one person (born in the Year of the Pig) conflicting with the symbol placements of their partner (born in the Year of the Ox)? Regards, Anneliese*

Dear Anneliese

The answer to you is yes, but only when it is in the corner of the room that belongs to the other animal in question. Thus the corner of the ox, which lies between 22.5 and 37.5 degrees of the compass, is the corner where you should not place, say, an image of the sheep, which is the natural enemy of the ox – this could hurt the ox corner. In the same way the corner of the pig (i.e. between 322.5 and 337.5 degrees) should not have an image of the snake, as this would hurt the pig corner. That is all you need to worry about. Everything else, including the activating of elements, should proceed as normal.

# Are separate bedrooms the answer?

*After reading Lillian Too's books, my husband has now suggested that we have separate bedrooms because of the fact that we belong to different groups. Lillian had mentioned in her book that, after having separate bedrooms, she and her husband became a lot happier and their relationship strengthened. My husband thinks it's the perfect solution, but I am sceptical about the idea. He says this way we can both be successful in our respective careers. He is a doctor and I have my own law practice. He is of the east group and I am a west-group person. What is your opinion? Mrs Tan*

Dear Mrs Tan

Well, if you feel so strongly about it, you should let your husband know. A lot depends on your age and the state of your marriage. Having separate bedrooms can help some people and hurt others. For those who have a strong relationship, separate bedrooms provide each with their own space, and if they also belong to different KUA groups, then need-less to say – from a feng shui perspective – the chances of having better feng shui for both parties is certainly increased. But in the end, of course, each to his own; different strokes for different folks.

# 9

# Love Angst

## LOVE DILEMMAS
## AND SOLUTIONS

Love gone sour? You're not the only one. The angst-ridden questions here are just a selection of hundreds I receive daily from people wanting less friction and more harmony in their partnerships. Of course, while feng shui can't change your partner's personality, it will help to maximize the good elements of your relationship – giving you both the best possible chance of success together. While you may not be experiencing the infidelity or constant arguments some of my correspondents are plagued with, you will find in the following pages feng shui cures that will improve any relationship – good water feng shui, for example, is key for ongoing commitment. Get your feng shui right, and you'll find that love really is the sweetest thing.

*Aunt Agga*

# We're newly-weds, but everything's going wrong

*I really like your page, but I have a real problem. Please help me. My husband and I got married one year ago (on 26 December) and since then we have experienced terrible opposition. It has been legal, financial, family and work. It is as if everything is working against us!*

*I think someone put a curse on our home and one on my husband, too. I want us to get what we have been working so hard for. How can I get the legal matters to work out right? Anything you could tell me would be greatly appreciated. Sincerely, Kathy*

*P.S. I noticed that when I put red carnations in my home, the energy changed. Should I keep putting them in the home?*

Dear Kathy

Oh dear, it sounds as if the feng shui of your house is really quite bad if everything is going so wrong. Firstly, can I ask if your main door is facing south? If so, then your problems are due to the bad Flying Stars (i.e. the "Five Yellow") in the south during the year 2000. Hang a six-rod windchime in the south near the door and this should make things better immediately. Please also remember that after 5 February 2000 you should remove the windchime and hang it in the north instead, because in 2000 the bad star has flown to the north.

Irrespective of whether your house faces south or not, you should try to "clear your space" immediately. Here is a simple method that is very effective. Open all your windows and doors and then, taking a mixture of rice and salt, walk round each room of the house in a clockwise direction and sprinkle the mixture against the walls, saying aloud as you move, "I am getting rid of all the bad energy, I am getting rid of all the bad energy..." If you wish, you can chant a blessing mantra as you walk around the room. Do three rounds per room. The rice grains are an offering to whatever spirit presence may be living in the home with you (all homes have spirits, so this is normal) and the salt is used to burn off all negative energy.

# Unhappily married...and I know our feng shui is bad

I have two questions. First question: as I enter my apartment I have a fairly large mirror facing the main door – as your book says not to have a mirror reflecting the door, what would you replace it with? And the other question is: I have a Chinese sword strung together by ancient Chinese coins hanging above the main door inside the apartment – is this good or bad?

My wife insists that both the mirror and the sword are excellent feng shui and, as she is of Chinese origin, I feel that she may be right, but I have my doubts. Although we have been married now for 10 years, ours is not a happy marriage and I would like to ask your advice for creating a more loving environment in the home. When I first

married my wife she was different; she was eager to please and very tender. That was in Hong Kong. Since coming back to live in the UK, however, our relationship seems to have soured. Perhaps you could pass on to me some of your wisdom. I might add, if you have not gathered already, that I am English. Thank you, Alan

Dear Alan

You really have more than two questions, and I shall try to be as helpful as I can, since I sense an underlying tone of sadness in your letter. Firstly, the mirror facing the door is probably causing you and your wife a great deal of bad vibes and stress. Remove it instantly and feel the difference. Change it for a painting – you should select the subject in accordance with the element of your door location. Secondly, hanging a sword of coins above the main door is also wrong. Hang it instead behind you in your office. A sword of coins should never be placed above a door, always behind where you sit. Finally, perhaps I could suggest that you check your bedroom and see if the sleeping directions of both you and your wife are correct, based on the KUA formula. Usually problems in marriage stem from sleeping with your head pointing in an inauspicious Eight Mansions direction. If you implement the changes here, the mood of your marriage will definitely improve.

After you have cleansed your home in this way, you may want to invest in a singing bowl to absorb any remaining bad energy and, more importantly, to create good energy. These space-clearing techniques work only temporarily and you should take more permanent measures to systematically study the feng shui of your home and then correct the features. Use Lillian's *168 Ways to Happiness* to do this.

## Impossible to live with, unless...?

*I would like to activate the north-west corner of my house to help my boyfriend's luck to improve. But the element that represents that corner is metal and I have just found out that my boyfriend's element is wood, according to the year in which he was born. Can I therefore still activate that room? I read that metal is destructive to wood. You know, if I don't do something soon to improve his luck, our relationship is going to deteriorate, since he is already becoming impossible to live with. Tammy*

Dear Tammy

Sure, you can use metal to activate the north-west. You know in Chinese astrology there are eight elements that make up the package of elements of a person. This is part of Four Pillars fortune telling which many people mix up with feng shui. So let's hope you do not make this mistake. From your letter, however, it seems to me that your problem has less to do with the north-west than with the overall feng shui of your home... Perhaps I could suggest that you systematically improve the chi of every corner of your living room, and particularly the corners that represent your boyfriend's auspicious directions. This will make life a lot more pleasant, happy and fulfilling than it sounds at present.

# We are arguing so much

*My husband and I have recently moved into our own home, but we have been arguing since we moved in. We have one exposed beam in the lounge room and I read that this is bad feng shui. Is this true, and could you give us any other hints for improving our relationship? Theresa*

Dear Theresa

It is not the beam that is causing friction between the two of you, although of course exposed overhead beams are bad feng shui. No, usually bad Flying Stars – what we call the "bullfighting, quarrelling stars" – cause arguments between spouses. These stars cause a lot of friction and fighting between occupants. If you find the quarrels getting worse try placing an urn of still water in the bedroom, but cover the water. If the water is not covered you might lose money or separate. Next please try to study some Flying Star feng shui to see if you can discover the exact source of your problem.

# I betrayed my boyfriend's trust – how can I get him back?

*My boyfriend broke up with me two months ago, then tried to come back a month ago, but we had a terrible argument and haven't talked since then. Among other things, he told me that he wanted to forget me and not talk to me any more. We love each other and I can't stop thinking about him. I really love him!! He is upset because I told one of his friends about a deception I knew of. He didn't want to get involved and doesn't forgive me for telling the truth. Can I do something to make him forgive me for being honest, and come back to me? Anonymous*

Dear Anonymous

Why don't you send him a love letter apologizing and saying that you really want him back again. Then place a red dot about 1cm. (1/2in.) in diameter in the middle of the back of the letter. This should help the letter carry some potency. Another method is to place his picture facing yours and then place two sheets of mirrors to sandwich the two pictures together. Let the mirrors face outwards.

# Fish ponds and fidelity

*We are about to buy a lovely property in the middle of a nature park, and I hope you can help me with a question. There is a beautiful fish pond in the park very near the house. I read in a book that is not good to have a pond on the front right side of the house entrance. Does this mean the right as you face the house or as you exit from the house? Anonymous*

Dear Anonymous

   This is the right as you face outwards, standing at the front door. The bad effect of a pond on the right-hand side is that the man (i.e. the husband or partner) usually tends to develop a roving eye. In severe cases, such a feature can cause the man to have a second family outside the marriage. A pond on the right-hand side thus has the potential to cause tragic unhappiness in this day and age. Imagine your partner telling you one day that he has a second family with another woman! So my advice is to be careful.

# My boyfriend has bad feng shui – will this affect our relationship?

*I'm wondering if you can help houses, other than the one that you live in. My boyfriend lives in a house where the relationship corner contains the toilet! If I place some crystals and encourage him to keep the seat down, will this help prevent our relationship going down the toilet? Liza*

Dear Liza

   Ask your boyfriend to keep the south-west of his bedroom energized with a cluster of crystals. Do not place anything inside the toilet and certainly not crystals. The love energy there is already afflicted, without you further strengthening this affliction.

# 10

# Bedroom Woes

## FENG SHUI FOR BETTER LOVE AND SEX

In this chapter, we deal with bedroom woes – in terms of the basics for good bedroom feng shui if you're starting out. We also cover your universal questions on mirrors, water, flowers and stairs in your personal sanctuary. These feng shui afflictions may be responsible for good sex gone bad – or maybe sex that is disappearing completely. Good bedroom feng shui is vital for undisturbed sleep and passion with your partner (if the two aren't incompatible!). Start with the belief that love and work in the bedroom just don't mix. Cover up your computer, mirrored wardrobes and televisions. Next, banish your water features and fresh flowers. To find out if windchimes will make your sex life magical, read on...

*Aunt Agga*

# Will bedside lamps cause a strain in our marriage?

*I am getting married in December and am renovating my room right now. My original plan was to put two wall lamps behind my bed for reading purposes and two extra side-table lamps beside the bed. But some people tell me that having lamps above the bed will cause a strain on the marriage. Is this true? They also say that having four lamps is inauspicious. I am quite confused. Can you enlighten me on this point? Thank you, Patrick*

Dear Patrick

Such rubbish!! Please proceed and enjoy your marriage. Placing lamps in the bedroom – especially red lamps in the room of newly wed couples – is usually a symbol to energize for babies. The only thing is not to overdo the red or the lighting. Too much yang chi can be harmful, but for young couples lamps are wonderful.

# Stairs and columns in my bedroom

*In my bedroom my headboard faces south and there is a staircase directly to my left going to the third-floor attic. Also, there is a staircase going down to the first floor that I can see from my bed, as there is no wall. There are also two support columns, one in front of the bed where the wall used to be and one beside the stairs. How do I minimize the bad effect of the stairs and columns? Thanks, Linda*

Dear Linda

This sounds like a rather badly afflicted bedroom. Stairs and columns all around you signify disturbances to your sleep, and they are also not beneficial from a feng shui viewpoint. Many things that you do will be blocked. This is the point about bedroom feng shui. When columns and structures cause disturbances to your sleep, it usually means that your projects, career and businesses will get stalled; and your relationships will encounter problems. I suggest that you camouflage the pillars with furniture or screens. As for the staircases, try to slow down the chi moving up and down the stairs by hanging windchimes above the top and bottom landing.

# Mirror facing the marital bed

*Could you please answer one question for me? My husband and I have our ups and downs, but we are reasonably happy. However, our marital bed is facing a set of mirrored glass doors on a wardrobe, with its foot to the mirrors. And I cannot change the bed from this position. Is there some cure I can use? Tricia*

Dear Tricia

Yes. Can you install a curtain to cover the mirror? It is much better to be safe now rather than sorry later on.

# Roses and water

*My question is regarding water in the bedroom. My master bedroom is in the marriage enrichment area of our home and the décor is primarily cream. I love the look of red roses in my bedroom, but I'm concerned that you advise not to have a water feature there. Would I be better off placing the flowers elsewhere? By the way, I live with my mother and I am friendly with a man whom I have known all my life. He is a close and good friend and he is also single, like me. He visits me a great deal, but we are not a couple, if you know what I mean... He has never shown any romantic interest in me, although he knows I am terribly fond of him. Do you think my red roses are preventing this relationship from blossoming into something deeper? Thank you for your help, Mary*

Dear Mary

Red roses are fine. They are not considered a water feature. However, if you want romance to blossom, why don't you consider peonies rather than roses? If you still prefer roses, do make certain that the thorns have been carefully removed before displaying them. Long-stemmed thorny red roses usually cause relationships to fizzle out. In any case your problem is not the roses. What you are lacking is family and marriage luck, so I would suggest that do something to bring a burst of yang energy to the platonic friendship and turn it into a passionate relationship instead. One way to do this is to enhance the lighting in your home and especially the south-west corner. Next, paint the south-west wall of your living room a bright red or yellow. This should at least jump-start the romance. And for good measure, hang a double-happiness sign there as well...

# Magenta all over

*My bedroom is painted and decorated in a beautiful shade of magenta, which I like very much, but my friend (who is a big fan of yours) has suggested that this might be too excessively yang. She says that all the men in my life will find me too much! I do not know what she means, but my relationships with men are usually not very satisfying. Do you think it is due to the décor of my boudoir? Chantal*

Dear Chantal

Your friend is not wrong. When the bedroom becomes excessively decorated with too much yang colour, the energy becomes overwhelming and overpowering. If the bedroom belongs to a married woman, she will dominate the relationship and eventually even break up the marriage; if the bedroom belongs to a single woman, her relationships will rarely satisfy her, in that the men in her life will always seem to be lacking in energy. To balance the intensity of magenta, perhaps the carpets, curtains and drapes can be made in a more yin colour, like light blues and off-whites. So, Chantal, my dear, lighten up the energies in your bedroom and you will get more satisfaction from your relationships.

# We don't have sex...and our bedroom is in my Total Loss direction

*Our master bedroom is placed in my Total Loss direction, and we have been living here for two years now. Is this why my husband is no longer interested in me sexually? I hate to think so, but recently he has taken to coming home very late and sometimes he even stays out the whole night. We are childless and although in the early years of our marriage he was keen to start a family, now he says that he is too old. I am wondering what to do. We used to have a mirror facing the bed, but I have removed it. Still my husband seems very aloof and distant. Please advise me what else I can do. Cheng Gaik*

Dear Cheng Gaik

Your situation is obviously bad. Sleeping in the sector of chueh ming (Total Loss), as you are doing, will eventually cause you to lose all that is near and dear to you, including in this case your husband. You do not say it, of course, but it sounds as though your husband is having an affair. All the signs are there. But the good news is that he is still trying to hide that fact. This shows he still has some feelings left for you. So my advice is for you to do something immediately. To start with, redecorate! This will change the energy very effectively. Select another bedroom and do it up really nicely. This not only changes the energy that surrounds your marriage, but will also give you a chance to position the beds and your sleeping directions in an auspicious manner, based on the KUA formula. Make up any excuse you wish to get your husband to agree. Let him sleep with his head pointing in his family direction. You will be amazed at the change you see in him.

# Missing marriage corner

*About a year ago, without knowing about feng shui, I bought a house in Los Angeles, California, after moving from Boston. Now I read from your book that my new house has the marriage corner missing. My girlfriend and I broke up after living in this house for five months. Before that we had been together for nine years.*

*I cannot believe that feng shui can be so powerful. So my question is: can I install a mirror to re-create the missing marriage corner? Do I need to cover the whole wall – if so, the cost would be too expensive for my limited budget. Please advise. Jack*

Dear Jack

I agree that using a mirror to remedy a missing corner can be expensive. But it is also the most effective remedy, as long as the mirror does not reflect a staircase, a door or a toilet. And yes, you will need to cover the entire wall. Another solution would be for you to strongly activate the marriage corner of your bedroom (i.e. if it is not missing). This is one of the fine points and lesser-known secrets of feng shui. This would compensate for the missing corner in the whole house. Or you could place a light outside where the missing corner would have been.

# Water in the bedroom

*Can we place a water feature in the bedroom? According to Lillian Too's feng shui books, she advises that no water feature is to be placed in the bedroom. Please confirm. Thanks, Randy*

Dear Randy

A water feature in the bedroom means placing an aquarium, a small pond or fountain near the bed...and while this may make for attractive décor in a magazine, in real life the feng shui of the sleeping area will be seriously afflicted. Water near the bed usually causes loss in different areas of one's life – loss of money, of loved ones and of opportunities. Some traditional feng shui masters do not even like having mountain scenes that show waterfalls hanging in bedrooms. They say that even this sort of feature is bad in the bedroom.

# Sloping walls in the bedroom

*I'm writing to you because I'm moving to a new house, and the bedroom I'll be in has sloping walls. Not only that, but they slope in my best sleeping directions. They slope on both sides of the room – east and west. The front door of the house is north, while the back door is west. I'm a west-group person. The north-west section of the back of the house is missing. Is this house all bad luck for me? I don't need any more bad luck, as I have no good heaven luck at all. Can you help me? Sincerely, Terry*

Dear Terry

If you feel so bad about this house, why are you moving into it at all? Surely if you are getting these bad vibes it would be better to look for another house? In any case, to sleep in a bedroom with sloping ceilings is not a good thing at all. If you have no choice, you can try to raise the energy with lights and clever positioning of the bed, but if you do have a choice, I would say don't move in at all.

# Master bedroom at the end of a corridor

*We have just bought a flat with a corridor and the master bedroom is at the end of the corridor. There are two bedrooms on the right side of the corridor and also a guest bathroom on the right side. Could you tell me if there is any remedy, as I have read in Lillian Too's books that occupants of the master bedroom will quarrel a lot if it is located at end of a corridor. Anonymous*

Dear Anonymous

Yes, it is not good feng shui to have a bedroom – or any room – located at the end of a long corridor. It is like having the entrance to the room attacked by a poison arrow. And, since this is inside the house, you should not hang a Pa Kua mirror to overcome the harmful straight vibes of the corridor. If you hang a Pa Kua symbol inside the house it does more harm than good. The best thing to do, therefore, is to try to literally slow down the invisible energy that moves along the corridor towards the bedroom. So hang paintings on the walls, and hang a mirror to add depth to the corridor. Also hang crystals and lights to keep the corridor well lit. All these solutions will distract and slow down the chi.

# Windchimes in my bedroom for a better sex life?

*Is it true that if there is a toilet in the north-west of the bedroom one should hang a windchime and then one's sex life will improve? I was told this at a seminar I recently attended, which dealt with feng shui and love. But a friend I made at this same seminar also told me that windchimes attract spirits and ghosts into the bedroom. Now I am confused and do not know what to do. I dare not ask my husband as he does not believe in feng shui. Please help me, Monica*

Dear Monica

Oh dear, please do not believe all that rubbish about windchimes. They do nothing for your sex life, believe me, and certainly they do not attract ghosts or spirits. Lillian Too says that she has been hanging windchimes in her home for over 20 years and not once has she had the pleasure of meeting a ghost! What is important to note, however, is that if you hang windchimes in your bedroom – for whatever reason – you should always make sure that they are not hung above the sleeping figure, and that they are not hung too high up. Windchimes work just as well when hung lower down.

# An irregular-shaped bedroom

*We sleep in an irregular-shaped bedroom that has several corners missing. I feel very disoriented and I have read that one way of correcting this is to have a wall-mirror. But I also read somewhere that mirrors in the bedroom cause problems with feng shui. Please advise, Marilyn*

Dear Marilyn

Yes, irregular-shaped bedrooms are not as balanced, and therefore the chi is not as fluid and smooth. Missing corners are usually remedied very effectively with mirrors, but in the case of missing corners in the bedroom it is better to tolerate the missing corners than to have a mirror that reflects the bed. I usually like to recommend the use of furniture to camouflage irregular-shaped rooms.

# My boyfriend has a real problem

*I would like to seek your help with my boyfriend. For the past few months he has been having trouble sleeping. He is irritable and always in a bad mood when he wakes up in the morning. Maybe this is because he is finding it increasingly difficult to have sex. Each time we try now it is unsuccessful. I have told him it is all right, that I do not mind, but that only makes him angrier with himself. What can I do? Can feng shui be used to correct his problem? Betty*

Dear Betty

Impotence is usually caused by other problems – or so I have read. In Chinese tradition we seldom use feng shui to correct impotence. Generally we use Chinese herbal cures, as there are herbs (like ginseng) that are said to be really good for such problems. But these days the West has discovered Viagra. Have you asked your boyfriend to try this?

# Four-poster beds

*Is it auspicious to sleep in a four-poster bed? Thanks, Anonymous*

Dear Anonymous

It is neither auspicious nor inauspicious. But it is a good idea to make sure that nothing too dramatic lies above your head when you sleep.

# Should I use a crystal or bamboo flutes?

*I would like to check if what I've been doing is correct. Our bedroom has a slanted ceiling in one part of the room (our apartment is located on the second floor). The bed is not directly positioned under the slanted ceiling (it's a small room). I have hung a small crystal in the middle of the room, hoping to get rid of some of the "shar chi". Do you think it's a good idea, or should I use bamboo flute instead? Esther*

Dear Esther

For slanted ceilings neither crystal nor flutes will be of much help. The best thing is to use lights to "raise" the energy of the part of the room where the ceiling is lower. Shine the light at the ceiling so that it is lifted up symbolically.

# My wife is besotted with her career
# ...and not me

*My problem is perhaps a common one, but it is that my wife is now besotted with her career. She is so involved in it that she has lost interest in me. Now she is always too tired and too busy for me. It has been like this now for about eight months, and we used to make love at least once a week. Now it seems as if she is not even interested in my advances. What shall I do? My work is as important as hers, but I still find time for her... Shall I change the bed?*
*Kam Chuen*

Dear Kam Chuen

It sounds as if she is sleeping with her head pointing in her career and success direction, which keeps her busy and motivated, while your sleeping direction is probably not as intense for you. It is also possible that her "family" corner is not active enough. What you can do to make your wife focus more on the home and family, and less on the office, is to activate the south-west – the place of the matriarch. Use crystals and earthenware jars and place them in the south-west of your living room. This will make her focus inwards. If this still does not work, you might try to reposition the bed. This shifts the chi and will cause her to take stock of her life.

# Redecorating with horses in the bedroom

*I'm planning to redecorate my bedroom and I would like to have the wall behind my bed decorated with a glass etching of six horses. This will be conceived like a Chinese painting. My questions are:*

1. *Is it okay to have six horses instead of the normal eight horses?*
2. *Is there any specific direction that the horses should be facing in relation to the bed?*
3. *Are horses generally appropriate for the bedroom?*

*Thank you, Cheng Siang*

Dear Cheng Siang

Six horses are not suitable, as the elements clash... Horses are best when placed south in the living room, but always looking in and never looking out... Horses in your bedroom placed above your bed would be horrendous. Especially when they are shown running – they would appear to be trampling all over you... So my advice is for you to think of something else, rather than horses. Even though they are auspicious symbols, one has to be careful what one places in the bedroom as decoration.

# Peonies in the bedroom

*Can I have a picture of a mountain peony with two butterflies hanging in my bedroom? Anonymous*

Dear Anonymous

Peonies in the bedroom are excellent for young women of marriage-able age. They are less suitable for middle-aged or older couples. They only cause the men in the marriage to develop an eye and an appetite for some sweet young thing! My advice is never to hang the peony inside the bedroom unless you are still very young.

# How can I dump my other half?

*I have been in a relationship for the past seven years which I no longer want to be in, mainly because the sex has been really bad. What can I do to get myself out of this mess? So far I have put a photo of us together (cut in half) in the south-west of my living room. I have hidden it under the fax machine so that no one sees it. Can you help? Christine*

Dear Christine

Have you heard of separation and divorce? And if you are not married, just tell him it's over. You really do not need feng shui to dump a guy! No need for such a ridiculous ritual, either!

# Picture depicting water

*You said that a water feature, such as a waterfall, in the bedroom is a big no-no. What if a picture shows a boat on water, like a lake with houses around it? I have two pictures like that on either side of the window. I believe they are on the south side of the bedroom. I really like your advice column. Thank you, Lisa*

Dear Lisa

I wouldn't hang the pictures, if I were you. Water in the bedroom suggests loss. So why take the risk, if it is so easy to cure?

# 11

# You and Yours

## FENG SHUI FOR YOUR FAMILY

With a family under one roof, no matter how small or extended, it can be a real challenge keeping everyone happy. You may be caring for young children, elderly relatives or sharing with friends, only to find that your good direction is your husband's worst, or that your rivalrous teenage sons are east and west group – but they have to share the same room. Feng shui can calm the chaos. You can change the sleeping directions of your children for sibling harmony, or activate the south-west corner with gold-painted stones to boost respect for a mother. From getting your children to do their homework to using the Chinese gods for luck, here's how you can enjoy a successful family life.

*Aunt Agga*

## Bringing luck for IVF treatment

*We have been having a hard time conceiving a child and the doctors said that I will have IVF (in vitro fertilization) treatment, probably in February. May I do something to increase the luck? Many thanks, Muriel*

Dear Muriel

Really, the best thing is to activate your husband's descendants' luck by sleeping with his head pointing in his nien yen direction. This is based on the KUA formula of Eight Mansions feng shui, which can be worked out from most of Lillian Too's books.

## Can the laughing Buddha or the Chinese unicorn help us have children?

*Hello Aunt Agga*

*Can you please help? My husband and I very much want to have a baby, but we have had no success. I am told that the Chinese unicorn can help, or a Buddha with children. Is either of these true? Can you help with any advice? I would be very grateful Thank you, Christine*

Dear Christine

Sorry to disappoint you, but no, the Buddha carrying children cannot help. Nor can the Chinese unicorn. What can help is the solution given in the answer to Muriel. This is for the husband to sleep with his head pointing in his descendants' luck direction. If you want to enhance the chances of conception, place an elephant in the bedroom.

## Bathroom in the children's sector

*I'm writing on behalf of a friend who's worried because her bathroom is in the children's sector on the Pa Kua. Do you have any recommend-ations to counteract this? Thanks, K.L.*

Dear K.L.

Place a mirror on the door to the bathroom, so that when you see the mirror, the bathroom visually disappears.

# Clashing elements

*My wife and I are deciding whether to have a baby in the year 2000 (metal), due to potential conflict with me, because I was born in August 1965 (wood). Metal destroys wood? My wife and I had good feng shui when our first baby was born on 28 January 1995 (wood) – she brings good luck to us. What do you suggest? Does it matter if the baby's element conflicts with mine? Jason*

Hi, Jason

The Year of the Dragon is always an auspicious one in which to have a baby and 2000, being the Year of the Golden Dragon, is considered to be even more auspicious for families who are blessed with a baby. But yes, being a year when the controlling element of the heavenly stem is metal, 2000 does clash with your element and thus could cause you some problems. But this can easily be remedied by introducing the word "water" into the name of your baby. The water will then weaken the yearly metal, while simultaneously enhancing your wood. So I would say: go ahead and have your dragon baby. If it is a boy it will be most auspicious and will be a cause for celebration.

# How can we produce a boy?

*Is there any feng shui secret that can help give us a boy? My husband comes from a traditional family and there is quite a lot of pressure that our child should be a boy. Thanks, Anonymous*

Dear Anonymous

Well, according to a certain feng shui formula, if you conceive during certain days of the month you will get a boy and on other days you will get a girl. This formula is generally based on whether the day of conception is a yin or a yang day, based on the Lo Shu Flying Star formula. Yin days beget girls and yang days beget boys. I have never tried this particular formula, so I cannot say for sure how potent it is. There are also other old wives' tales about the determination of the child's sex, but I would say that these fall in the realm of superstition rather than feng shui.

# Family portraits

*I want to take a family portrait. We are a family of five. Is the triangular shape the best for us? Also, should my father be at the top of the triangle, since he is the head of the family? Thanks, Cheryl*

Dear Cheryl

Yes, the triangular shape would be excellent, since this represents the element of fire, which produces earth, and as I'm sure you know the number five is of the earth element. So the elements are in balance. And definitely your dad should be at the apex of the triangle.

# Getting someone out of our life

*How can we get someone out of our life who is always jealous of any success or happiness that we have as a family? This person has even filed a lawsuit against us and is causing us much heartache. Thank you, Laura*

Dear Laura

For this kind of problem I always recommend that the south-west corner of the living room (which is the social area of the house) is appeased by placing a bright light, a crystal or something red there. The south-west governs relationships luck. But usually severe problems of the type referred to here suggest that you might be suffering from what I would call the "bullfighting shar chi" of afflicted Flying Stars. What you can do is either take on the difficult job of doing a Flying Star analysis of your home or place an urn of still water in the living room. This can symbolically absorb and dissolve the fighting stars to some extent.

# Can feng shui encourage marriage luck?

*Dear Aunty Agga*

*My name is Sara and I have been seeing David for two years now. We have become close and I am very happy. However, to date, David is reluctant to talk about marriage and kids. Can anything in feng shui help me?*

Dear Sara

If you are asking if feng shui can make him more marriage-minded, then no, feng shui cannot control what people will or will not do. But if you are asking if feng shui can energize your marriage luck and enhance your chances of getting married, then the answer is yes. Place a pair of mandarin ducks and a bright light in the south-west corner of your living room. If David is meant for you, and you have the heaven luck to marry him, then this could be the catalyst that makes him think seriously about a commitment. If not, then you could suddenly meet someone else who is meant for you.

# My child refuses to study

*I wonder if there is anything you can recommend to make my 12-year-old be more conscientious in his studies? Presently, unless I "bribe" him, he will not even sit down to do his homework. I always have to promise a trip to the cinema or the toy shop before he sits down to do any work. In this day and age, when school results are so important and everything is so competitive, I really worry. My husband seems to be less concerned than I am. Is there anything I can do feng shui-wise? Thank you for your help, Wanda*

Dear Wanda

Yes, there is something you can do to make your son more interested in improving himself. Perhaps you can arrange his sleeping position so that his head is pointing in his personal development direction while he is sleeping. This is based on his date of birth, and you can study and learn this KUA formula in any of my books. It is a powerful formula that will bring good luck to you and your family, including your son. Meanwhile I should discourage you from resorting to bribery, since it is really not good in the long run.

# Shelves directly above my daughter's desk

*I read that having shelves directly above a child's desk hurts their concentration. Is this true? If so, how can I overcome this, as my daughter indeed has a shelf above her desk right in front of her. Is this why she is having difficulty concentrating? She also cannot seem to do well in her studies, even though she tries really hard with her work and is in fact quite conscientious. Jackie – a concerned mother*

Dear Jackie

I strongly urge you to get rid of the shelves above her. This is an example of a terrible poison arrow. You will see the difference as soon as you have them dismantled. This was exactly the reason my nephew was doing so badly at school. As soon as we dismantled the shelves, his grades started to improve almost immediately. So don't try to place things such as windchimes and crystals to block them. Poison arrows are best removed. It is only when you cannot do anything less that you look for easier remedies.

# Kids sleeping in bunk beds

*Is all right for kids to sleep in bunk beds? If so, does it matter if they sleep with their heads in opposite directions? Thanks for a great job! G.*

Dear G.

It's fine. But do calculate their good directions based on their KUA formula. Then let both sleep according to their respective good directions.

# A difficult child

*My 11-year-old is very difficult to deal with at home and at school, although it is carelessness and naughtiness rather than anything more malicious that causes the problems. Many American friends of mine have suggested that he should be on medication for Attention Deficit Syndrome, but I have always resisted this.*

*I think his elements are out of balance with the rest of the family. He is a fire rabbit, annual KUA 4, monthly KUA 7 in the house of Ken. His elder brother is water pig, annual KUA 8, monthly KUA 7 in the house of Sun. I feel I should be able to use the complementary position-ing of the two boys' monthly numbers to help, but can't work out how. I am a metal rabbit, female KUA 2, and my husband is a metal tiger, KUA 5. It feels like wood is exhausting all the earth around, and whatever support we give is never enough. Do you think feng shui can help? Anonymous*

Dear Anonymous

I am not sure I understand your references to monthly and annual KUA numbers. There really is no such thing in feng shui, as far as I know...so I shall have to pass on making comments. From your letter, I think you are making feng shui too complicated. The most effective thing you can do for your son is to let him sleep in a way that allows him to tap his best directions, based on his KUA formula. You calculate this from his date of birth... In any case, if you feel he is not in need of medication there is no reason to give him any.

# Colours for bedroom walls

*My daughter and I are both fire element people. Can we use pink for our bedroom? The toilet tiles in my room happen to be pink. If pink is not suitable for us, then what colour should we choose? Please help! Aileen*

Dear Aileen

Pink would be a good colour for you both, but there is always the danger of having too much fire. In the bedroom, while a light pink might be excellent for your young daughter, it might not be so suitable for you... Usually when women's bedrooms have an excess of fire, the yang energy becomes too strong and this can have a negative effect on their relationships with men. My suggestion is to have a light, off-white colour, which puts you in charge (because fire controls metal) without it being too obvious. If you were born in the summer months, then a light blue would be more suitable. This is because summer is also fire and then the excessive fire should be subdued with some symbolic water energy. Please note, however: a blue colour is fine, but not actual water.

# Staying with my husband
# for the sake of my children

*I have recently lost my mother, approximately six months ago. My marriage was unstable before and has got even worse now. I have three lovely children and am carrying on as best I can for their sake. I do love my husband, but he can be difficult at times and, as I am getting older, I feel that my patience is running out with him. I work night and day to make ends meet and give my children what they need. I would like us to live happily as a family unit, as – no matter what – they love their dad. I hope you can help me. Thank you, Meena*

My dear Meena

It is obvious that you love your family very much, and your mother must have been a great comfort to you. Probably you miss her and the moral support she provided. But with her gone, my dear, you are now the matriarch and you must be strong, not just for your children but also for your husband. Yes, he needs you, even though he does not know it. Men can be quite obtuse like that. So please hang on in there and you will be amazed how strong you really are.

Let me now give you some feng shui tips to strengthen the matriarchal energy in your home. This will help you considerably in many different ways. The place of the matriarchal chi is the south-west. So the first thing to do is to identify the south-west corner of all the bedrooms of the home and also the south-west of the living, dining and family rooms. Then systematically brighten this corner of the room. Move all the lights in every room to this south-west corner. Be very systematic and determined about this. Then place natural crystals in the south-west corner. If you find crystals too expensive, you can also place boulders, which have been cleaned, painted a golden colour and tied with red string. This activates the chi of the stones.

You will be pleasantly surprised by the result. Not only will you yourself feel stronger and more confident, but your husband will begin to respect you a lot more. Your overall luck should also improve.

# Bully at school

*I know that my question may sound absurd to you, but my son has a real problem at school and it has been getting increasingly difficult in the last few weeks. He is desperately afraid of a bully in his class and cries when I ask him about it. He has also made me promise not to say anything to the school. I know he is afraid, and so are all his classmates, but it seems the class bully has everyone so frightened that no one can do anything. My son has told me that even the teachers are afraid of this bully. Is there anything I can do? Please help, Rosie*

Dear Rosie

Your question is far from absurd. School bullies have always been a problem, and I know exactly how your son feels. But of course he is wrong to be so afraid. Bullies are usually great cowards at heart. If I were you, I would have a quiet chat with the school head teacher and, together with your husband, discreetly investigate the problem. In the meantime it would really be a help if you let your son wear some kind of protective amulet, if you can. Wearing a dragon pin on his body (hidden away) will give him more courage, and in his bedroom hang a picture of a mountain, or display the image of a dragon tortoise or a dragon horse. These are all symbols of protection that will help him overcome his fear.

# Bad luck in studies

*I have been experiencing bad luck for the past month in every aspect, especially in my studies. I would like to know how I could improve my luck in my studies. Is there any solution? Tom*

Dear Tom

Well, you might want to check if anything sharp, pointed or straight is pointing directly at you while you sleep or while you work. These are poison arrows that cause you to experience bad luck. As for having bad luck in your studies, you can overcome this by sitting facing your personal development direction under the KUA formula. This is called the fu wei direction.

# Difficulty conceiving

*We have been married for five years, but we have no children yet. We have been trying hard. For the last two years it seems that my husband has always had some minor health problem; headaches or the flu come and go. Is there any possibility that our bedroom has a bad feng shui? It is located in the south-east and our bed faces the south-west. Thanks, K.*

Dear K.

My advice is to use the Eight Mansions Formula which uses the KUA formula to determine auspicious and inauspicious orientations. This will enable you to discover the orientation of sleep that will best suit your husband's descendants' luck. This is the nien yen or family direction, and once you know what this direction is, you can position the bed in such a way that this orientation can be tapped. Next, you should also go out and check that there is no poison-arrow structure that is pointing sharply at the front door... If there is, try using another door. If there is nothing medically wrong with either of you, then feng shui can probably help solve your problems.

# We are adopting two boys

*My husband and I plan to adopt two boys. We have three birth sons of our own. We plan on putting a family room in the basement of our home, with an extra bathroom with a shower, sink, toilet and whirlpool bath. The main family room will have a gas fireplace. Any suggestions for colours and/or furniture placement? Are whirlpools recommended? I would like an area of peace and tranquillity for our family as we add two more members to it. Jane*

Dear Jane

That sounds very sweet, and I can tell you that what you plan to do is fine. Having a family room in the basement is excellent when you have so many children bringing good, old-fashioned yang energy there. Good luck with the two new additions to the family! Did you know that the Chinese believe that when you have five sons it signifies the peak of good fortune?

# Examination blues

*In Singapore, student life is highly competitive. We have two sons (non-identical twins), who are both sitting for their A-level pre-university examinations this year. These are important exams and it is vital that they get good grades, since both wish to make it to the top universities and also want to qualify for government scholarships. Our problem is that the brothers are competing with each other so much that they are barely on speaking terms with one another. The atmosphere in the house is terrible.*

*I do not want to comment on anything and have been pretending not to notice, but last week they almost got violent with each other. I do not want to disturb my husband about this and wonder if their intense rivalry is due to bad feng shui? They share the same room, but since they ignore each other one always sleeps on the sofa in the living room. Is there anything I can do to reduce this tension? There are still several months to go before the crucial exams. I am so afraid that things will blow up any time now and am at my wits' end.*
*See Eng*

Dear See Eng

Maybe the Flying Stars of their room are affecting them. Have you tried moving them into separate rooms? This might help. Or maybe a heart-to-heart chat with both of them? If you do not do something to diffuse the situation, they might do something stupid. This sounds like an extreme case of sibling rivalry and it indicates a disharmonious household. You might like to see if there are any beams or protruding corners affecting them. Also check their sleeping directions.

# 12

# Feng Shui Home Dilemmas

## LOGISTICAL PROBLEMS
## IN THE HOUSE

**D**id you know that there are good and bad house numbers in feng shui? You may have heard the story of a Chinese businessman house-hunting in San Francisco. He found the perfect home, but on departing discovered that the house number was 444. Unfortunately, the number 4 when spoken in Chinese sounds very like the word for death, so he turned the house down without a second thought. We can't all choose our house number, however, and if we did, we could end up living somewhere that had a great number – such as 168 – but had terrible interior feng shui! Here's where you learn how to display a good number, play down a "bad" one, and how to fix feng shui essentials such as correct placement of stoves and sinks, bedrooms and bathrooms. Pay a little attention to domestic detail and you'll make your home the hub of good fortune.

*Aunt Agga*

# Unable to move our door

*I am living in Singapore and have recently purchased an apartment that is due for renovation soon. Due to some restrictions, I am not allowed to move the position of the main door. My husband and I belong to the west group and our main and master-room door faces north. However, we are occupying the room that is in a good location according to our KUA number. Can you kindly advise what can be done to improve the situation, as the door cannot be moved?*
*Many thanks, Stephanie*

Dear Stephanie

If you cannot change things, you cannot change them. No point knocking your head against the wall trying to do the impossible. So instead of using the Eight Mansions personalized formula, you should instead learn to use and apply the Flying Stars formula which allows you to identify the lucky sectors of the apartment. In this way you can be sure of tapping the best luck that your apartment can offer each year.

# Front door and bedroom problems

*I've read in one of Lillian Too's books that the door plays a main part in feng shui. Please help me with the following, as I can't find the answers in any of her books:*

1. *My master bedroom opens to a double-panelled window at the entrance, and the exit faces the toilet door. What must I do?*
2. *My husband belongs to the house of Sun (east group) and KUA number 4. According to the KUA number, the main door is facing an inauspicious location. How do I reduce the bad chi from coming in, without changing the main door?*

*Thank you, Katie*

Dear Katie

Place windchimes between the toilet door and the bedroom door, and use curtains to cover the windows. As for the unsuitable main door, there is nothing you can do. But don't worry, because really in feng shui it is impossible to get everything 100 per cent correct.

## Two doors in a row

*My back-room door directly faces the front door. Is it okay to put a bookshelf instead of a screen in between them? Anonymous*

Dear Anonymous

Yes, indeed...as long as the chi is forced to slow down and take a deviation, this is fine.

## Long stairs stabbing the front door

*My parents have just moved into a house that they bought 15 years ago for retirement. I am a little concerned about a straight staircase leading up to the second level of the house when entering the front door. Is that something I should worry about? A concerned daughter*

Dear Concerned Daughter

Yes, unfortunately that is something you should worry about. Remember the Tsars of Russia? The whole family massacred and completely wiped out? Well, they had a long staircase facing their front door, just like the staircase you describe in your parents' house. I would tell them to move out again, or do something about it, such as reorientate the front door. I hope all goes well.

# My kitchen location is wrong – can you help?

*According to Lillian Too if the kitchen is located in the fu wei [the fourth good direction based on the Eight Mansions formula], the result will be no money, no longevity, forever poor. It so happens that our kitchen is in my husband's fu wei, and on the second floor of the house a toilet is also located in his fu wei. Can you suggest any cure for this. Thanks a lot, Tani*

Dear Tani

Well, surely you know that the only solution is to relocate your kitchen. There is no easy way to practise formula feng shui like this, but take heart: you can make up for this by ensuring that the oven mouth, or the source of energy that cooks the food of the family, is coming from an auspicious direction.

# Apartment feng shui

*In Singapore it is difficult to get, or even build, an ideal house based on feng shui concepts (form-school feng shui), especially since most of us are living in high-rise apartments. Since my best direction is north, is it all right if I live in the north-east part of Singapore (Total Loss, my inauspicious corner), but with my main door facing north? Anonymous*

Dear Anonymous

Indeed, yes... As we keep saying, in feng shui we cannot get everything right. It is not possible. You also need not worry because the orientations of your immediate space exert a far greater influence than the larger environment.

# Is a humidifier a water feature?

*I have just been finding out about feng shui and discovered this helpful website. I was reading the question-and-answer section and saw people asking about water in the bedroom, and I see that it is a big no-no. My question is: how about a humidifier? I use one all winter long because of the dryness, and really don't feel that I could do without it. Is it going to be a problem? I thought about putting it in the hallway right outside the bedroom, but this will make it cramped and it will have to have a long extension cord to try keeping it out of the way. Hope you can help. Anonymous*

Dear Anonymous

No, the humidifier is not a problem. So no need to worry about it.

# Mirror above the stove

*Years ago I read that you should put a mirror up above your stove to increase your wealth. So for all these years I have had the mirror above the stove and our wealth has increased slowly. However, we have experienced some difficulty with our youngest daughter. She is unhappy and seems without clear direction. Just recently I read in the Feng Shui for Modern Living magazine that to have a mirror above the stove could be dangerous. Anonymous*

Dear Anonymous

Yes, indeed, placing mirrors near the stove can be dangerous, especially if the mirror is reflecting a naked flame. Mirrors in the dining room are very auspicious, however, because here the mirror "doubles the food on the table", which symbolically also means an increase in wealth, because a wealthy family will always have plenty of food on the table. Some feng shui "experts", though, took this one step further and cooked up a new solution by recommending the placement of a mirror by the stove, on the basis that this would "double the food being cooked". What it does, however, is to double the fire, not the food (especially if the fire on the stove is a naked flame). Mirrors that reflect the stove cause problems with children and, in extreme cases, could even cause the home to burn down. Please remove the mirror above your stove immediately.

# Where do I eat in my studio apartment?

*I recently discovered feng shui and have made some big changes in my apartment. I do have a slightly unusual situation: I live in a large studio apartment with a separate kitchen (and bathroom). The wall opposite my front door is completely glass and includes two sliding glass doors. I keep the blinds closed over the glass door that is exactly opposite my front door and have hung a crystal on the inside of the door and a metal windchime on the outside. I separated my bedroom with two bookcases, but I do not have a dining area, so therefore I have no table to eat on. Do you have some advice for me? Warren*

Dear Warren

As long as you do not eat too near the sleeping area, it is fine. If I were you, I would place a dining table at the very front of the apartment.

# Dining room lower than living room

*My dining room is lower than the living room. I understand from reading Lillian Too's feng shui books that such a situation is bad or inauspicious. What can I do? Anonymous*

Dear Anonymous

Perhaps you might want to use the dining room as the living room, and vice versa?

# Poison arrow from pillar

*Where I sit there is a square pillar with one edge pointing to my back. I was advised to put a plant behind me, to block the shar chi from hitting my back, but this is not possible because there is no space on the floor near the pillar for a plant. But I could hang an artificial firecracker from the ceiling. Can I do this? What are your suggestions? Anonymous*

Dear Anonymous

In this case a plant works better. A firecracker is not suitable. Can you hang a potted plant from the top of the pillar?

# Which is my front door?

*We bought a house that has been renovated, and on the front of the house is a huge glass-enclosed playroom. This is where the entrance to my home is, and the glass structure has a door on one side and a sliding door on the other. It is north facing. When I have guests we let them enter through this door, while the sliding door remains closed most the time. When we enter and leave on a daily basis we do so through the kitchen door. Which is my front door? Thanks, Francis*

Dear Francis

It can of course be any of those doors that you use, but in feng shui a situation like this does not generate good energy. When even you cannot decide which is your front door, how can the good chi know which door to use when entering your household? So designate a proper main door and use it often. Then make all your calculations and feng shui based on this main door.

# Front door in death sector – help!

*Help me! My front door is in the death sector. What can I do to offset the ill-effects of its position? Thanks, Nikole*

Dear Nikole

What do you mean by the death sector? If you mean it is in the Total Loss sector, based on the Eight Mansions Formula, then the way to offset this is to make sure that you sit and sleep in accordance with your sheng chi direction.

# How can I sell my house quickly?

*I'm trying to sell my house
and wanted to ask if there was
anything I could put inside it,
or remove, to speed up the
sale? I have two Pa Kuas
outside my house. One is
facing south-east and the
other is west. Please help.*
*Anonymous*

Dear Anonymous

Hah! No wonder you cannot sell your house. With not one but two Pa Kuas outside your house, you are "pushing" people away. Much better to get rid of the Pa Kuas and then keep one bright light turned on at the back of the house. This will make it much easier for the house to be sold.

# Colours in feng shui

*We are renovating an apartment community. The plan, for now, is to paint the doors black. Does black have any meaning? And is this a bad idea? If so, what colours are auspicious? Also, if a colour like green is good, can you use any variation of green, such as sage green or olive green? Thank you for your help! John*

Dear John

Black is not always a good colour; you need to check several things before it becomes good. So when it is correctly done, it is excellent for wealth luck – but if bad, then it's really bad. Red is excellent and so is white. Green – any shade of green – is good, but a vibrant, growth-coloured green is better than a dead-looking green.

# Bathroom directly over the front door

*My bathroom is located directly over the front door, which I have read is not an auspicious position for a bathroom; it is also located in the north-west, my sheng chi. Short of relocating either the door or the bathroom, could you please give me some advice as to what I can do (I already make sure that the toilet seat is down and the bathroom door is closed)?*
*Lots of love, Cazza*

Dear Cazza

The best – and in fact the only – solution I can offer (apart from moving the door) is to place a very bright light shining upwards at the ceiling to raise the chi and push it upwards.

# Home above a former graveyard

*We are considering buying a flat in San Francisco. We recently found out that the property lies above what used to be a cemetery (in the years after the Second World War the graves were moved to a nearby community and the land was "reclaimed" for homes). In all other regards the home is beautiful (quiet neighbourhood, convenient, etc.). How does this affect feng shui? Best wishes, Joseph*

Dear Joseph

It was after all so long ago that you might be forgiven for thinking that it should not matter that much, although personally I would pass on living above a yin place like this. If you'd like to live there, however, it might be a good idea to undertake some space-clearing before moving into the new house.

# Side of aquarium facing the main door

*I live in a double-storey terraced house and the main door faces south, and this door is at the left-hand corner (when looking from the inside). I have placed my aquarium in the south-east corner. In it is a single arrowana, that is about 30cm. (1ft.) long. However, the side of my aquarium faces the main door. According to my friends, the side of the aquarium, which is made of glass, will deflect the main door and this is no good. If I do not use this area, where else can I put the aquarium? Anonymous*

Dear Anonymous

Well, you could surely rearrange the aquarium so that the main door is not afflicted? What is the use of putting a good-fortune symbol like the arrowana in place, only for it to hurt your front door?

# Main door facing my worst direction

*I have a problem. I have just discovered that my main door is actually facing east, which is my chueh ming (worst) direction, according to Pa Kua and Lo Shu. Is there any way of diverting bad feng shui, besides relocating the main door? Thanks, Anonymous*

Dear Anonymous

The best solution is to change the direction of your main door. If you cannot, then the only thing to do is to try and make sure that your other applications of the KUA formula are properly done.

# Overhead beams

*I've an overhead beam in my living room and would like to reduce the negative energy by hanging a crystal below it. Will it work if the crystal is hung by the side of the beam or must it be directly beneath? What's the most effective way of reducing the negativity of the beam without sacrificing the modern look that my apartment has now? Thanks for your help. Regards, Eric*

Dear Eric

In fact the crystal should be placed at the edge of the beam for it to be effective.

## Putting up house numbers

*I need to put up some numbers (21) at the front of my house – is there a specific way I should place them (i.e. slant them up or down)? Thank you for your help, Felicity*

Dear Felicity

    I guess you should place the numbers high up rather than low down and make them appear prominent.

## Burglaries

*There has been a spate of burglaries in our area recently. Is there a way of using feng shui to lessen our chances of being burgled, as our whole family is going away on holiday? Anonymous*

Dear Anonymous

    Definitely. Place a broom next to the front door, with the sweeping end up and the handle at the bottom. This is an old feng shui ritual to keep burglars away.

## Acceptable colours for rooftops

*We are in the process of having our roof restored – i.e. washed, chipped tiles replaced, sealant applied and finally resprayed in its original dark brown colour (the bricks on the walls are also dark brown). In one of Lillian Too's books she says that blue is definitely out and strongly recommends red. Although red is the preferred colour, we were wondering if the original dark brown was okay too? Anonymous*

Dear Anonymous

    Oh yes, brown is good. It is the blue that is most dangerous.

# Water fountain in an apartment

*I live in a small apartment and would like to know where it is best to put a water fountain and windchimes? Also, where do I place the bamboo flutes with the red ribbon? I need a little feng shui help, because I want good fortune to come to me and to my apartment. Anonymous*

Dear Anonymous

Place the fountain in the north; the windchimes in the north-west; and the bamboo flutes to block out overhead beams.

# Ivy plants

*Is it bad to use ivy plants that have three-pointed, dagger-shaped leaves inside the house – either as a live or a silk plant, or as a design on wallpaper, etc.? If not, can it be used it in a yard? Anonymous*

Dear Anonymous

As a wallpaper it's fine, but this plant is better outside the home.

# Apartment directly above the garage

*I write from Italy. I live in a small apartment 40 sq. m. (48 sq. yd.) on the ground floor. It is immediately above a garage. I know that it is not good to be above a garage. What can I do?*

*The bathroom is in the centre of the house. This is also a problem that I do not know how to solve. And the bathroom is almost in front of the entrance door. Kindest regards, Maurizio*

Dear Maurizio

Living above a garage is considered inauspicious because it is interpreted as living above a vacuum. For most of the time a garage is left empty. So if you can hang a picture of a small mountain in the garage, this symbolizes the vacuum being filled up with earth, which is also excellent grounding energy for your apartment. The bathroom in the centre of the home causes disharmony among family members. Place a large stone sculpture, or simply a boulder, in here to stabilize the chi; this should be very helpful.

# Windows directly opposite the front door – does my luck rush out again?

*I'm currently living in a new estate and all the flats here have their main doors opening on to a straight row of windows. Does this mean that luck will rush out of those windows the minute it enters the house? How do I cure this? Anonymous*

Dear Anonymous

Yes, it does mean that, so it's not auspicious at all. But it is not difficult to overcome. Invest in some heavier curtains and keep that part of the window that faces the main door permanently closed.

# Site location for a new house

*I have bought a site for a house. When I first started to learn feng shui, it enhanced my appraisal of the site: it faces south/south-east (a valley); it is on a hill, with a wide, open view; it is protected by a small hill in the north and west directions...*

*Then I discovered the Eight Mansions Formula. Since my KUA number is 6, my home should face north-west (the back part of the site) and, for a house on this site, it is almost necessary for it to open to the fantastic view of the south and south-eastern landscape. What should I do? Forget the site? Best wishes, E.C.C.D.*

Dear E.C.C.D.

No, if you like the house so much, by all means get it...but you are KUA 6 person, for whom the best direction for the main door is not north-west, but either south-west or north-east. So can you make it so that the main door faces south-west, but the side window opens to the panoramic view that you want? A lot depends on the site itself – and on how clever your architect is – and do not forget the Flying Star natal chart. People with the best chance of getting excellent feng shui are those who build from scratch...but to get the best from feng shui you should check that all the auspicious directions for you and your family can be incorporated into the home design.

# 13

# Plagued by Bad Luck

## WHAT TO DO WHEN EVERYTHING SEEMS TO GO WRONG

Have you ever thought that it couldn't get any worse – and then it did? Here's a global view of bad luck from every quarter. Although, of course, we can't expect untold riches without effort, some of the correspondents in this chapter have experienced acute disappointment – losing jobs, homes, lovers and money simultaneously. I've dispelled the superstition around some of these crises – "unlucky" opals, for example, are not to blame – and explain how a destructive cycle of events can be halted. Paint your door green to keep money coming in, sleep in your best direction, use the double-happiness symbol – whatever the problem, feng shui will help cure the malaise of misfortune and attract the abundance you need.

*Aunt Agga*

# Financial anguish

*We're desperate! We have tried many feng shui remedies to help correct our financial situation, but this year things have become hopeless. At present we are way behind in our rent, car payments, and well – you name it and we're behind. We can't imagine what we are doing wrong.*

*This past weekend we widened the entrance path to the house – the driveway is sort of a circle. The gardens are beautiful, but we removed the potted roses that were along the entrance path, in case the thorns were creating problems. The entrance door faces north, but the room looks to the west. The bathroom and toilet are in the south-east corner.*

*I published a book this year, but borrowed the money to do so, which compounded our financial problems. The book has been slow to take off, but I shall be setting up a web page as soon as some money comes in. There seems to have been a blocking energy in regard to the book, and to financial progress in general. I hope you can help. Warmest regards, Wendy*

Dear Wendy

Oh dear, I wish I could help, but all I can really do is point you in the right direction. So I would advise you to check your directions according to the KUA formula, and also to check the Flying Star charts of your home. It sounds like Flying Star afflictions to me...so it is worth investigating that.

# Getting mentor luck

*I have energized the north-west sector of my house (it is also the north-west sector of my living room) with a six-rod windchime (hollow type) and my hi-fi set for the past year. However, I don't seem to have got any mentor luck yet. I think it is because this sector is at the lower end of the sloping ceiling. How can I counter this? (Using bright light will conflict with the element of this sector.) Anonymous*

Dear Anonymous

You are right – using bright lights here destroys the element of metal. Perhaps you might wish then to strengthen the metal element with a "mountain of gold". This would be a pile of rocks painted gold.

# Being a good husband and father

My name is Harvey, I am 38 and I have a wonderful relationship with my wife of 14 years. I also have a wonderful son of 10. My problem lies in the fact that for so many years I have struggled through life and tried to provide the best for my family, but it never seems to be enough. Bad luck just seems to attach itself to my soul and I cannot shake it off... I am not a believer in religion, being born into a Sikh family of Asian origin, probably because I never had time to dedicate to it. But I was pleasantly introduced to the science of feng shui two years ago through reading an article on the subject.

I do not want millions – I just want to be comfortable. We moved the bed to an auspicious direction; and the toilet was surrounded by plants, because it is in the south-east sector of our home and there is only the one, so it has to be used. I believed this would absorb the shar chi created. We have a Pa Kua mirror outside the front door in the south-west, and we have had the garden trimmed of overhanging trees and placed crystals and frog windchimes where recommended in Lillian Too's books. We even have a fish tank with nine fish (one black). Even with all this, our bad luck still has not diminished by any great amount, even though the house has become a comfortable place to live in. I became self-employed 13 years ago and have not seen what you call "good times". We had to sell the business because financially it was becoming a burden – could it have been the Pa Kua mirror hanging outside the Chinese restaurant pointed in our direction? At that time I did not know what it was. The financial burdens of that business are still with us and sometimes we can just about make ends meet.

I get great inspiration from reading Lillian Too's books and your column, and from carrying out the enhancements to improve our energies, but sometimes we feel that it just temporarily lifts our spirits... I know it sounds as if I am looking for drastic results, but if only the feng shui would work, as it has done for many others cited as examples in Lillian Too's books and elsewhere. Please advise with any recommendations that may help to achieve my goals.

My date of birth is 7 January 1961. Element: metal. My wife's date of birth is 27 February 1966. The house has a south-west front entrance and an east back door. Very grateful if you can help in any way, Harvey

Dear Harvey

The south-west is unlucky for you, based on your date of birth, but is very good for your wife. The Pa Kua hitting your door has enhanced the bad luck for you. So I strongly recommend that you try to use another door if you can and, if you cannot, to buy a tree (or a tall bushy plant) and place it in front of your entrance door. This will block off the bad vibes from the Pa Kua across the road, and will also dissolve the afflicted and damaging chi coming from the south-west. If you still cannot do these things, then I suggest you paint your front door a bright, fresh green colour. This signifies the wood energy which will dissolve the afflicted earth energy coming from the south-west... Things should improve considerably after you make these changes.

## Bad spirits

*Could you please give me advice for coping with the bad spirits that follow me? Thanks, Audrey*

Dear Audrey

How about carrying an amulet or starting to chant some mantras? If you like, here is a very powerful mantra of the compassionate Buddha. Chant 108 times each morning and night, and whenever you feel afraid: *om mani peh me hone*. This is a wonderful mantra, which when you chant it with a good heart and pure motivation will also make you feel at peace with the world. It helps clear all obstacles facing you.

# My husband may be suicidal

*I desperately need help – I think my husband is suicidal. He lost his job three months ago, after being with the same company for nearly 20 years, and has since been unable to find even temporary work. Because of me trying to hold my family together, my business (which is a book and magazine shop) is going under. My son is trying to study for his matriculation exams and we are desperate for money.*

*Please advise us what to do – I have bought three-legged frogs, Chinese coins and have done all that I can think of in my simple way. Can you please help? Our birth dates are:*

*Mine (Elaine): 5 January 1956*

*Husband (Anthony): 15 March 1952*

*Son (Adam): 21 December 1981*

*I just need to know what to do and how to get over the next three months – I am desperate and do not have the money to call in a feng shui expert. Please help. With thanks and God bless, Elaine*

Dear Elaine

Oh dear, you sound very harassed indeed. Staring at the sort of future where your source of income is uncertain can be very frightening. So I really hope that feng shui can help you quickly. No need to bring in a feng shui expert. At a time like this you must not spend your money foolishly. Instead, the first thing to do is to enhance the feng shui of your husband. From his date of birth I can see that his KUA number is 8, which makes him a west person and his best direction for getting a job and improving his finances would be south-west – so start by letting him sleep with his head pointing to the south-west. Do your best to achieve this, but if it is not possible, then try the north-west direction. Also, locate either the south-west or north-west corner of your home and let him sit, sleep and work there. Ask him always to sit facing the south-west when he applies for a job or goes for a job interview. Just concentrate on this and don't worry about the symbols...

As for you, your KUA number is 3, which makes you an east person and your best direction is south, so everything I am recommending for your husband also applies to you, except that you should use your per-sonal best direction. Do the same analysis for your son to help him in his studies. When you are more comfortable financially, you can start to enhance your feng shui in other ways.

# Are opals back luck?

*I was told that opals are bad luck, if you wear them and they are not your birthstone. Is there a feng shui cure for opals and the people who love them? Anonymous*

Dear Anonymous

Who said opals were bad luck? Cheers.

# Windchimes bringing nightmares

*My dad placed a metal pagoda windchime in my bedroom. He placed this according to the Flying Star analysis that he studied from Lillian Too's book. He said that my room has the main star of two and the Chor-Sin star of five, which spells bad luck. He placed one in his bedroom, too. The windchime is quite near the fan in both our rooms. The problem is that my family and I have found it difficult to sleep because of the sound. I have nightmares every night and cannot get a good night's sleep. What I hear from other people is that windchimes bring bad chi. Is this true? My dad said that in his room the main star is five. Lillian Too's book recommended that a windchime be hung in rooms with the numerals two and five. He did so because there was a quarrel and disrespect among family members. Is he doing the right thing? Anonymous*

Dear Anonymous

Your dad is definitely doing the right thing in hanging the windchimes. They are a powerful antidote against harmful Flying Stars, except that the windchimes need not be hung so high up. Place them lower and in a corner, so that they do not distract you. Let them do their work quietly, otherwise a remedy becomes a problem. We hang our windchimes so they are barely noticeable; windchimes don't have to tinkle to work!

## Divorce and other problems

*In a quiet moment at work yesterday I found the website for World of Feng Shui – a subject that I have been extremely interested in for about a year. I get very confused, though, and while I do my best to follow all the advice, sometimes I come up against conflicting explanations.*

*My KUA number is 9 and my best direction is the east. I was born in the Year of the Ox and, from reading the horoscopes etc., I seem to be heading for a bad year! I have just had the worst two years of my life, and I am desperate for a turn-around.*

*I have recently become divorced and I am still fighting to keep my house. The whole process has taken two years! And just when I think I am about to succeed, another delay occurs. It is very frustrating and I sometimes wonder if this is just the way my life is going to go. The divorce was not my idea, but nevertheless, at the end of the day when you have been married to someone for 27 years and give him all your heart, and then you discover that they don't love you anyway and never have done, it takes a lot of your confidence away.*

*With the help of feng shui I have managed to regain some faith in myself. My difficulty is that, just when I decide what is right for me in feng shui, I read something that turns everything around! I have been using the east as my best direction (until I read another web page!); north is my second best direction, so should I now use that direction? Please let me know.*

*I have put crystals around my house and painted auspicious calli-graphy in gold on red material (something I really enjoyed doing). I hope to meet someone else one day, to whom I can give all my love (and hopefully receive some back), as I do not want to be on my own for ever. I enjoy sharing things. I have two children, both now grown-up, although my daughter still lives at home with me and we are very close, but she has her own life to lead. I have used the 49-day ritual and nothing happened. I have bought coins, three-legged toads and done everything suggested in Lillian's books – and also in the magazine – but still nothing. I am really ready to give up... Sorry to go on a bit! Look forward to hearing from you, Mary*

Dear Mary

You sound so sad... Don't be sad – first of all, work on yourself. Be strong; shake off this feeling that your life and fortunes are determined by anything outside yourself. Even when you read that certain years and directions are not good for you, remember that this is all relative... You know, the Year of the Rabbit is said to be very bad for roosters, and guess what: Lillian is a rooster and she shrugged her shoulders and said, "Okay, so it's bad. I shall simply lie low then." Never make your state of mind weak by being subliminally defeated.

Next, use feng shui as a tool to improve your happiness, not as a crutch. How? By not depending on it mentally. Just do what you want to do to energize, and then forget it. Don't sit waiting for the luck to come. It will come, and here are a few excellent tips to use. But don't go overboard by using too many things...just these will do, okay?

1. Place a picture of a double-happiness symbol in your bedroom – use one with a red background or one that has the word itself in red.
2. Place a water feature – like a goldfish bowl – in the north sector of your living room (not the bedroom).
3. Place a light in the south-west of your garden (if you have one); if your garden does not face south-west, never mind – place it in the south instead.
4. Place a picture of a mountain behind you where you normally sit.

These are simple, symbolic feng shui enhancers to use and they are enormously potent. Good luck. But remember, in the end, if you are strong mentally and emotionally, you will feel a surge of confidence inside you, which will enhance your chi considerably. So be strong!

# Cheated of money

*I am presently in the US as a student. I have been here for two years and have moved four times. I work during the summer to help pay for my studies. However, I was cheated by the company I was working for and lost $550 for nothing. I am wondering if it could have been due to my feng shui? Can you help? Best wishes, Jack*

Dear Jack

I wouldn't know for sure, but some questions might elicit possible answers. Did you have any water in your bedroom or any pictures of water? Did you have any poison arrows hitting your sleeping position or your front door? Were you sleeping with your head pointing in one of your inauspicious directions? Or did you have a toilet in the south-east of your living space? Answering yes to any of these questions suggests you suffered from a feng shui affliction, which caused you to be cheated.

# Personal auspicious and inauspicious directions

*I wonder if I could consult you regarding personal auspicious and inauspicious directions? How do you handle the situation with the inauspicious directions? I'm especially worried about north-west which is my mentor area and my Total Loss (chueh ming) direction. My KUA number is 9 and my inauspicious directions are:*

1. *South-west = lui sha (Six Killings): I'm 50 and single, so obviously that explains that.*
2. *West (children and creativity) = wu kwei (Five Ghosts): I don't have children, but I very much appreciate creativity... How can I activate it? Or can't I at all?*
3. *North-west (mentors and helpful people) = chueh ming (Total Loss): this sector is extremely important, yet for me it's Total Loss. Can I activate it or not? At the moment I have angels there and a light, as well as a six-bar windchime.*
4. *North-east (education, knowledge, learning) = ho hai (Unlucky): my kitchen is there, although I would love to educate myself spiritually, but for a long time I have felt blocked. I read and philosophize, but it's very "narrow".*

*Can you please advise. Best regards, Eva*

Dear Eva

Perhaps you are reading too much into the inauspicious directions. You are an east-group person and so the west-group directions are bad for you. This means that you should try never to sit facing or sleeping with your head pointing in these directions. Also, try to have all doors facing at least one of your good directions. But what you have done is combined two different schools of feng shui and that is not correct. Thus, just because north-west is your Total Loss direction doesn't mean that you cannot activate it to encourage helpful and influential people to come into your life... What it does mean is that you should not face that direction when working and that you should try not to sleep in a north-west sector of your home. But yes, you can activate this same sector and benefit from it... Hope this clarifies a very important point.

## What is wrong with my personal feng shui?

*I have been so strapped for cash since last year, after I had to shut down my business. I had to give up my apartment (because I could not pay the monthly rental) and am now living in my sister's apartment with her fiancé till I can afford a place of my own again. They seem to be doing okay, financially and otherwise, and are always more than ready to help me whenever I need it, but I have been living off their hospitality for so long now that I feel very bad. I've been trying to look for work, but I only seem to be successful in getting low-paid jobs. What is wrong with my personal feng shui (since the feng shui of my sister's house can't be so bad, as she and her fiancé are both doing well)? Jacey*

Dear Jacey

There is nothing wrong with your personal feng shui, I am sure, but there may be something wrong with your heaven luck; or your mankind luck. You know, if you really feel bad about depending on your sister and her fiancé, then you should take a job (however low the pay), at least until you can find something better. You could try some inner feng shui, through meditation, and some mental spring-cleaning. This could clear blocks that cause you not to succeed at what you do now. Sometimes blockages in life when things go bad are only preparing us for something better just around the corner.

## Money problems

*I am the main breadwinner of the household and recently, since moving into this new flat, I have experienced lots of money problems. I am sleeping with my feet facing south-east, and my head is along the same wall as the door leading into the bedroom. My bedroom is blue. Can you let me know if there is anything wrong with my sleeping position? Harry*

Dear Harry

From the little information you have given me it is hard to tell if your sleeping position is causing you your money problems. Please check your auspicious directions and see if you are maybe sleeping with your head in the wrong direction. Also check for harmful beams or corners that may be hitting you. Money problems are usually caused by the main entrance door being afflicted, and rarely by bedroom sleeping positions. So I would recommend that you investigate the feng shui of your main entrance door.

## Fish tank in the bedroom

*In Lillian Too's books it says not to have a fish tank in the bedroom. Is this why I am having so much bad luck in my life? I have one – I had read somewhere else that it's good to have a fish tank in a room. I am confused! Aunt Agga, please help, Janet*

Dear Janet

Please do remove the fish tank as soon as possible. It will cause you to lose your money – and sometimes even your loved ones.

# Changing fortunes

*A few days after I moved into the apartment I now live in, my career – which had been going very well – took a turn for the worse and eventually I lost my job. My love life came to an end, and my finances totally dried up. I bought a few of Lillian Too's books and discovered the following: my front door which is in my living room, is in the south-west sector of the apartment (my KUA number is 1, and that's my chueh ming or Total Loss direction), and it faces north-west at 290 degrees (my lui sha or Six Killings direction). My bedroom door is in the south-west corner of the room, facing north-west. The kitchen is in the north sector, and the stove faces north-west at 290 degrees (both the gas conduit going into the stove and the oven mouth).*

*I read on your home page that the south (my nien yen) should not be enhanced for 1999 and 2000, so this meant that for two years I could not even tap my good direction. So my question is: how about the east then? I would like to get a fish tank to place in the south-east sector. My apartment has an area of about 60sq. m. (72 sq. yd.), so would a 68-litre (15-gallon) fish tank be too big? Thank you so much for having such a great column! Cathy*

Dear Cathy

Oh dear, sorry we initially missed your letter which is the kind I consider to be most urgent. So apologies for this delayed response. Before going any further I would say: please try to move out of your apartment... It is very bad to suffer from a double-whammy, like your situation, and that is why you are experiencing all this bad luck. Now, if you cannot move out for whatever reason, then please try to use another door. While you can sleep in a west bedroom, you must make sure that you sleep with your head pointing either east, south-east, north or south. As the south was afflicted by the Five Yellow in 1999 and by the Three Killings in 2000, it had to be avoided during these two years. You still have three other directions to choose from. And yes, you should energize your south-east, which is your sheng chi or most auspicious direction. So sit facing the south-east and yes, bring in the fish and water and place them here. It's not too big a tank. Please make sure you implement these things immediately.

# 14

# Exterior Feng Shui

## DRAGONS, TIGERS, TURTLES AND MORE...

Exterior feng shui is all about nature's chi, the "wind and water" that is the literal translation of feng shui. Water is a uniquely powerful activator of good and bad fortune, so begin by assessing your water features, such as fish ponds, fountains or swimming pools and always place them to the left of your property. This stimulates the patronage of the dragon, the celestial animal that represents wealth energy. Check out the "bright hall" effect, too – this is, ideally, an area in front of your home that is brightly lit, brimming with flowers and foliage, that acts as a wealth-attractor. Lift the energy in dull yards with outside lighting, plant trees to protect your home and family – and you'll see your garden, finances and relationships bloom.

*Aunt Agga*

# Where is the dragon?

*I am really confused. When standing inside the front door, facing out, is the "dragon side" to the left or the right of the house? Then what about people saying the dragon is in the east? Thank you, Chandra*

Dear Chandra

The general consensus among experts on landscape feng shui is that the land on the left of the house (from inside looking out) is the "dragon side", even if it is not the east according to the compass. This definition is for the purpose of defining good and bad contours and slopes around your home. So the dragon side (the left side) should always be higher than the right side.

# No turtle protection

*We have a wonderful view from the back of our house – overlooking a valley – but alas, we do not have any protection from the turtle. There are simply no hills behind us, let alone a turtle hill. Does this mean that we lack protection? I have two windchimes at either end of the deck and there is a split-rail fence at the edge of the ridge. Any further suggestions? Thank you, Connie*

Dear Connie

If you really cannot see hills in the distance, and if the back of the house is a valley, then yes, it does mean that you lack the protection of the turtle. Since you obviously enjoy the view from the back, may I suggest that you reorientate your house by changing the main door. Either use another door or create a new one, which allows you to place the valley either by the side or by the front of the house. You can use this as an opportunity to design a new door that is more auspicious for you, by tapping one of your good directions.

# Is my Russian olive tree a poison arrow?

*Question: the front door of my home is facing south-east. There is a single large tree in line with this door in the south-east sector of the yard, and it is 21m. (70 ft.) away. The trunk is not straight: a curved, graceful line is created. The tree is rectangle-shaped with light-green, pointy, slender leaves. It's called a Russian olive tree. If I understand correctly, this tree is not a poison arrow and does not need to be removed. Is this correct? A so-called feng shui expert told me, "That tree must be removed because it is in front of your door." Katie*

Dear Katie

The tree is curved, it is away from the house, and it is rectangular with small leaves. Sounds wonderful! My advice is that it does not sound like a poison arrow at all, but is in fact excellent, since it is in the south-east direction. It is bringing you loads of good luck. If you cut it down you will lose the good chi brought by the tree, so you are correct.

# Feng shui in different cultures

*Although feng shui doesn't regard itself as localized within a specific region, how does the philosophy of feng shui in architecture translate to the separate regional cultures? Anonymous*

Dear Anonymous

Oh my, what an academic question! All I can say is that it is best to approach feng shui in a practical manner and not worry too much about the cultural philosophies behind it. In any case, when feng shui was first "invented", the world was a far different place from today, and just as architectural concepts have had to keep up with the times, so too has the interpretation of feng shui concepts.

# Tiger v. dragon

*I have just purchased a large, solid concrete dragon and positioned it on the corner of my verandah to the left-hand side of my front door (when standing inside looking out) and a cat statue (tall, narrow and made of concrete) which represents the tiger, on the right-hand side at the other corner. My front door faces north, so the dragon is in the west and the tiger in the east. To my left (west) is a rise in the land and to*

my right (east) the land slopes away. My question is: do I have these animals in the right position in relation to: a) the east and west locations they should be in, and b) the slope in the land. Jerry

Dear Jerry

Yes, indeed you have. In landscape feng shui the left-hand side is always the dragon side and the right-hand side is always the tiger side. So what you have done is correct. However, inside the home, when you wish to energize the real east of your room, place a dragon on the compass east. This is because in the practice of compass-formula feng shui we use the compass, but when it comes to building and energizing according to the lie of the land, we place the dragon on the left.

## Telephone pole

I have a telephone pole directly opposite my front door. It is on the other side of the street. Is this affecting me, and how do I ward off its bad influence? Margie

Dear Margie

This would be a tiny poison arrow and its effect is quite insignificant, but if it bothers you, hang a small windchime with five rods in front of your door, or plant a tree to block the telegraph pole.

## Bad location for our new house – can we remedy this?

*The house we are planning to buy is located near an electricity sub-station, separated by a road. The sub-station is facing the left-hand side of the house. I read in a feng shui book that sub-stations give off negative chi to the house. Another feature of the house that I'm not comfortable with is that the land in the back yard is slightly lower than the road. What can I do to remedy both these features? Jill*

Dear Jill

    You can block the bad vibes from the sub-station by planting a tree with lots of foliage to fend them off. As for the back land being slightly lower, again you can plant a few trees or install a tall light behind, to lift the energy.

## Pillars blocking the entrance

*My husband and I are moving to a new house (rented) in three weeks' time. We need your advice. At the entrance of the house are three pillars (brick). The owner planned to build gates, but in the end didn't. Will this stop prosperity from entering our house? Anonymous*

Dear Anonymous

    Yes, I'm afraid so...but these are also easy to correct. This is not a good façade to have, but you can soften the effect of the pillars by placing decorative plants next to them.

## Driveway slopes down from the house

*My house is situated on a hill, so the driveway slopes down from the house. I read that this is bad feng shui for the family's good fortune. Are there any remedies? Anonymous*

Dear Anonymous

    Well, it is believed by many feng shui masters that this causes all the family wealth to flow out... The best way to remedy this is to place a high, bright light at the bottom of the driveway. This symbolically lifts the chi.

# Are my house plants affecting my feng shui?

*Is it important where I place my house plants? I was born in Year of the Rooster (1969) and am sharing a house with a guy and a girl born in 1972. Right now I have a box and (three) containers of herbs which have been along the south window. My studies are great, but my job and love life are not going as well as they could! Also, someone else in the apartment has planted white lilies outside my bedroom window (which faces west). These are the only things that have changed around the house. Thanks! Emily*

Dear Emily

   Sounds good, from what you describe. The white lilies outside your west window are good for you, too. If you want a better love life, plants won't do much to help, although they don't hurt.

# Wall blocking my front door

*I recently moved into a town house that has a two-storey wall (the side of another unit) 3m. (10ft.) from my front door. What can I do to help correct this blockage? Tim*

Dear Tim

   I would not worry about the wall. With 3m. of space you can create a "bright hall" effect by making a beautiful garden with a lawn and flowers, and even a water feature. I have seen homes with excellent feng shui that had an even smaller space to work with.

# 15

# Feng Shui
# Facts and Figures

## TECHNICAL KNOW-HOW

Y ou don't have to be Einstein to grasp feng shui formulas. You can use them to calculate your Chinese birth sign, your KUA number and all your good and bad directions. Learn how to fit your house plan on a Lo Shu grid, find out if there's a difference in feng shui for the southern hemisphere...and, strange though it may sound, learn to use a compass correctly. Given that I'm inundated with many questions relating to the use of the compass in feng shui, I have included several key questions dealing with the difference between facing a direction and being located in a direction. For the technically-minded, I also include questions on Flying Star (which addresses the dimension of time in feng shui) !

## *Aunt Agga*

# Calculating KUA numbers
# in the new millennium

*I am currently studying in Canada and have run across a problem with calculating KUA numbers. I currently use the method outlined in Lillian Too's books. I have been told that this method will not work in the new millennium. Is this right? Surely since this wonderful art has been practised for so long, this is not the first time that practitioners have run across this problem. Should I change the formula used? Thank you for your time, Susan*

Dear Susan

The formula used and recommended by Lillian in all her books was devised by her as a shortcut method of getting the KUA number, from where one can then refer to her tables to find out one's good and bad directions. With the changeover to 2000 and the 21st century, all that's needed is to amend the formula slightly for those born in the new millennium. For all of us, once we know what our auspicious and inauspicious directions are, they never change – even in the 21st century. For those of you who wish to calculate the KUA number of babies born in 2000 and beyond, just substitute the number 9 for 10 for males and the number 6 for 5 for females. Let us see some examples:

**For boys**

KUA number for a boy born on 3 June 1989 - the formula would be:
Take the last two digits of the year of birth 8+9 = 17 and then 1+7 = 8
Then 10-8 = 2, so his KUA number is 2.
KUA number for a boy born on 3 June 2000 - the formula would be:
0+0 = 0, then instead of 10-0 we have 9-0 = 9, so his KUA number is 9.

**For girls**

KUA number for a girl born on 6 April 1992 - the formula would be:
Take the last two digits of year of birth 9+2 = 11 and then 1+1 = 2
Then 2+5 = 7, so her KUA number is 7.
KUA number for a girl born on 6 April 2000 - the formula would be:
0+0 = 0, then instead of 5+0 we have 6+0, so her KUA number is 6.

# The Eight Mansions and landscape schools clash – which is more important?

*What should I do if, in using the Eight Mansions KUA formula, my toes are pointing directly to the toilet? My other best position is either facing the door or the window. Please advise, Jamie*

Dear Jamie

The texts always say that the form school is more important than the compass school, simply because poison arrows and afflicting physical structures cause feng shui to be bad, even when directions may be auspicious. Thus the landscape school is more important than the Eight Mansions Formula. So in your case you have to choose between the toilet, the door and the window. I would say that, of the three options facing you, the window option is the least problematic.

# Different feng shui methods

*I don't quite know how to figure out the difference between the compass direction and the direction represented by the Pa Kua trigram. My entry gate is situated in the Pa Kua area represented by knowledge (facing compass direction north-west), with the wooden door also in the same Pa Kua area but facing compass direction north-east. From here, I can draw out the nine squares on my apartment with no problem.*

*When you mention keeping a terrapin in the north part of the house, is this the compass north or the direction represented by the Pa Kua (i.e. career)? On the compass, the north part of my house is in the Pa Kua area represented by health/family. However, the Pa Kua north (career) is west, according to the compass. I would be grateful if you could enlighten me. Reena*

Dear Reena

The method you describe is the one used by Prof. Lin Yun's Tibetan Black Hat Sect of feng shui. In authentic Chinese feng shui we always use the compass to identify the direction and compass sectors. So all my recommendations are based on the compass, not on the method described by you. So when I advise you to energize the north with a terrapin, to encourage good income luck from your career, I am referring to the real, magnetic north as indicated on a compass. Hope this clarifies things.

# Flying Star

*To determine the natal chart of my house, do I use only the compass direction (one of 24 sub-directions) of the front door that faces the street? Or do I use only the sub-sector in which the front door is located (e.g. front door faces N1, but is located in the third sub-sector of the north-west corner of the house)? The second example would mean that I use the NW2 and 3 natal chart, and the first example, the "compass direction method", would mean that I use the N1 natal chart, giving a completely different Flying Star for the house. Thank you again, Michael*

Dear Michael

Of course in Flying Star feng shui we use the direction to compute the natal chart, and after that we use the chart to investigate whether the sector housing the main door is as auspicious as it should be, or whether it can be improved. That is how feng shui masters make their recommendations. See how, once you know this, all becomes clear?

# What makes a good Luo Pan?

*So far I have read many feng shui books, but now I would seriously like to try out some feng shui for my home, and would like to purchase a Luo Pan from a local store. However, I do not know how much a good and effective Luo Pan usually costs and what I should look out for when buying one. Could you give me some tips? Sincerely, Jonathan*

Dear Jonathan

The Luo Pan is the feng shui masters' compass. It is a very special feng shui tool, but the Luo Pan that you buy from the local store or Chinatown is worth nothing! A good Luo Pan must contain the authentic formulas and an excellent compass. Its production must have been overseen by a good feng shui master. Such Luo Pans, which are never mass-produced, cost at least $400–500 and, believe me, they are worth their weight in gold. The best person to buy a Luo Pan from is the master himself. Authentic feng shui masters of advanced levels of knowledge always have their own personally designed Luo Pans. Lillian Too has just completed her hand-made Luo Pan which contains six major formulas, check this out at www.fsmegamall.com.

# Which is the front of my apartment?

*In my pursuit to find balance in my life, I have begun to study feng shui. However, I seem to be running into walls when I try to put the ideas into practice. I live in an apartment where one door opens to the living room and the other door opens to the kitchen. The kitchen door is the most-used door, because it leads off the driveway/parking lot of the complex. My living-room door faces a courtyard. By architectural standards, this is the front of the building. As far as feng shui is concerned, which is the front? I am looking forward to enhancing my life with these principles. Thank you for your assistance, Henrietta*

Dear Henrietta

I would use the door that is most frequently used by you as the main door, although the other door – the one facing the courtyard – is best. This is because the courtyard is deemed the "bright hall", which is most auspicious. The kitchen door should be considered the back door. But check the directions of the two doors against your own personal directions as well. In the end, you must be the final decision-maker on all this. Select the door that brings you the best luck.

# Confused by having to place south on top

*I am so confused on how to use the Pa Kua directions... Does this mean that I have to interchange north with south, even though the compass says it's north? Please explain to me briefly. Thank you, Louie*

Dear Louie

No, you do not have to change the directions in the application of feng shui principles. We follow exactly what the compass says. Even though we place the south on top in our illustrations, this does not mean that we are changing north for south. If that were the case, then we would also have changed east for west –and there would then be no end to it. So placing south on top is only a writing convention adopted by the Chinese... In reality, when we speak of north and south, we are referring to the same directions as Westerners are. So beginner practitioners need only invest in a good Western-style boy scout compass. As long as you can determine your orientations, i.e. know where north and south are, etc., you can practise feng shui.

# Northern and southern hemisphere feng shui

*Is feng shui applied the same way in both the northern and southern hemispheres, given the differences in seasons? Or should I flip the directions? Laura*

Dear Laura

You really should not flip the directions for the southern hemisphere...if you do, you will get all your feng shui completely wrong. Those who have been going to the southern hemisphere advocating this are quite irresponsible, as it has served to confuse many people in Australia, South Africa and South America.

Worse, it has also caused a lot of misfortune and done genuine, authentic feng shui a grave injustice. This is because feng shui depends on much, much more than just sunlight and heat – feng shui takes account of many different factors. So to answer your question: no, there is no need at all to flip the directions, and you can read Lillian's books (and other books) with an easy mind.

I might add that masters of feng shui who KNOW the advanced formulas know instantly why the directions must NOT be flipped. It is only those whose knowledge of feng shui is shallow, incomplete and superficial who advocate flipping the directions.

# Merely north or "true" north?

*I am constantly confused with one question that I feel, when answered, will ease my frustration of understanding feng shui. Of course I know which way is true north. But when you refer to specific directions, such as "the south wall of your living room", does this mean that if I am standing in the entrance looking into the room, and I am at the north, that the wall directly across from me is south? Is this correct – or am I supposed to find the true south of the room? Another example is my front door: as I stand in it, looking outside, I am facing the west. This would mean that north would be to my right: correct? So when I lay out the map, placing north at my entrance, I get it all turned around and west becomes north? I know you always enter from the north – but it is not always true north – correct? See how confused I am, Sig*

Dear Sig

Well, all I can say is that you make yourself confused and in the process end up confusing even me...but at least I know what you are asking. Firstly, when we refer to the north or south, we are referring to magnetic north, as indicated on any good compass. And guess what: north is always north, no matter where in the house you stand. Okay?

Now, when we talk feng shui, we always refer to two things – the compass direction and the compass location. In Chinese lingo these are sometimes referred to as the facing direction and the sitting location.

When we investigate the direction of the main door, we stand at the door itself, then we look out and read the direction in front. This is the direction that the door faces.

When we want to demarcate the compass sectors of the house, we stand in the centre of the house, then find out where the north sector is; from there it is easy to find all the other sectors.

Hopefully this will make you a lot less confused.

# Afflicted by the deadly Five Yellow

*If the deadly Five Yellow is in the south, does this mean all rooms in the south or the south of every room? And if no activity is allowed in the south (e.g. no music, etc.), then what happens if we hang bells or windchimes (as is frequently advocated) and they chime and make a noise? Will this worsen the bad effects of the Five Yellow? Anonymous*

Dear Anonymous

Good question. Generally speaking, your logic is correct. But according to the texts on Flying Star, the sound of metal against metal is said to be a most powerful cure. And when we say the Five Yellow is in the south, it means the south of the house and the south of every room. By the way, the south was afflicted by the Five Yellow in 1999 and will be again nine years from then, as the stars move in nine-year cycles.

# Problems fitting my house on a Lo Shu grid

*I have a problem. My house is not aligned as a rectangle along the south–north axis, so I cannot overlay the Lo Shu grid on it. The front is facing south-west and, as such, how do I overlay the Lo Shu grid on it? Furthermore, my house is rectangular in shape and so shifting the numbers to align with the direction may not be proper. Tom*

Dear Tom

Lillian's house also faces south-west and it is also rectangular, rather than square. It is easy... Look at a conventional Lo Shu square and then transcribe the matching numbers over to your house's Lo Shu square. The front centre square is now south-west, so to the left is south and to the right is west. Good, now fill in the Lo Shu numbers in the matching squares: 2 in the south-west grid; 9 in the south grid; and 7 in the west grid. If your house is rectangular, then make each of the small grids rectangular as well.

Easy, huh? Surely you did not think that only square houses can enjoy good feng shui?

# 16

# Creating Abundance and More

### Includes everything else you need to know

This chapter shows just how broad the reach of feng shui can be – and how enticing. You may have wondered if windchimes have to tinkle to work, where to place your cat's litter box or how many arrowana fish to keep... For the more pragmatic, learn how to energize with crystal balls in the south-west and north-east, how multiples of nine fish bring financial good fortune, and how and where to place your dragons and turtles. Activating good directions with these feng shui energizers can fuel your love life and finances, so choose and place them with care. Good luck!

*Aunt Agga*

# Elephants in feng shui

*I read in Lillian Too's book of feng shui symbols that the elephant is one of the auspicious animals to place in the house. However, there is no indication whether the elephant's trunk should be raised (as if in a trumpet for joy) or otherwise. I read in a book written by a Filipino that the elephant's trunk should always be raised; also that elephants should not be placed facing the main door. Please advise me about your views on this. Thanks, Karyn*

Dear Karyn

Elephants can have their trunks up or down. In Chinese texts on the subject the elephants are always shown with the trunks down, as the elephant is regarded as a benevolent creature that brings descendants' luck. In Thailand the white elephant is said to be so rare and so scarce that just sighting it brings good fortune. An elephant with its trunk up, by the way, is not a sign of triumph, but rather a sign that it is about to attack.

# Feng shui and football

*My local football team is currently having its worst run in living memory, although last season they were fairly successful. I'm sure the poor results are connected to the recently opened stand which for the first time in the club's history has enclosed the southern end of the ground. The northern end of the ground has no stand, so I believe that the north–south flow of chi energy is now blocked. How can feng shui help with something as large-scale as a football ground? Please let me know. We are desperate for some decent results! Adam*

Dear Adam

I don't think your team's bad results are due to the stand blocking the flow of chi. Last year had the Five Yellow in the south...so if your stand was erected this year, you must have provoked the negative energies of the Five Yellow. By the way, this year has the Five Yellow in the north, so if you are thinking of building another stand, leave the north side alone. Build elsewhere. Good luck with the football!

And by the way you might want to design an auspicious T shirt and logo incorporating victorious colours for your team. That might just do it!

# On-line shopping for feng shui products

*I write from Copenhagen, and would like to know where I can buy good-fortune symbols? I know I can't find these symbols in Denmark, so would be willing to buy them on-line through mail order. I would be very grateful if you could help me with this. Best regards, Thomsen*

Dear Thomsen

You can purchase great feng shui products and good-fortune symbols from many on-line feng shui sites now, but do be careful of the prices that you pay. Sites that I can recommend are Dragon Gate Palace and the Geomancer – they take credit cards on-line through a secure server, and they are also honest and reliable in terms of pricing and quality. Check out the other on-line stores that we recommend by visiting http://www.wofs.com. We update our recommendations regularly.

# Sewing good feng shui

*I am preparing to move into my own apartment with my husband next year. As my hobby is sewing, I have sewn quite a number of large pictures. One of them is of eight horses galloping, and another is of different types of dogs (about six or seven) smoking, gambling and drinking at a poker table. Besides these, I have a few other pictures depicting a house with a pond, with ducks swimming on it. I am currently sewing a scene of a yacht floating on the sea and some trees surrounding the environment. My concern is: would there be any problem if I hang all these pictures in the living room? Please advise. Thank you very much, Lindy*

Dear Lindy

None of the subjects mentioned by you sound anything but good. It would be a great idea to turn this into a small business by putting good-fortune symbols into your pictures and selling them. Think about it. We would be delighted to be of help to you.

## The silver "wish box"

*I heard a feng shui consultant on the radio mention something about a silver wish box; supposedly, you write down your wishes and place them inside the box. Can you tell me a little bit more about this practice? Also, where should I place the box for best results? Would it make sense to place the box in the section pertaining to the wish – but what if you have wishes relating to multiple sections? I would like to hear your thoughts... Thank you! Kellie*

Dear Kellie

Yes, I've heard about this, too. How wonderful if feng shui could create magic like this. I suppose this must be a variation of Taoist magic, huh? Well, try placing a silver wish box in the north-west corner of your living room and see what happens. The north-west is big metal (hence silver) and it also stands for heaven luck, so that could be the source of this new ritual? I like to keep an open mind about such things and shall certainly try it out myself to see if it works.

## A yellow dragon

*I just bought a lovely yellow jade dragon. Where should I place this, and pointing in which direction? Is it okay to leave it in the bedroom? I remember reading from some feng shui books about the green dragon and white tiger, but mine is yellow. Is this okay? Alvin*

Dear Alvin

Yellow dragons are earth dragons, and they can be extremely power-ful. Place these earth dragons in the south-west or north-east – which are of the earth elements – and let them bring you great relationship and diplomacy luck. They should indeed cause you to be most effective in the PR area of your life. Certainly you will become more popular.

# What is the right number of fish to keep?

*I have just built a lovely fish pond at the front of my home and placed eight goldfish and one black fish in it. But I need more fish to eat up the algae and to keep it clean. Can you please tell me: how many of each colour can I add to keep good feng shui? Thanks so much for your help! Fond regards, David*

Dear David

You are like me. I love lots of fish... Keep them in multiples of nine to ensure that they are auspicious, although having said this I have to confess that I have loads of fish of every variety.

# Crystal balls

*I would like to know where to place a yellow crystal ball in my bedroom. Is it true that when we wear crystals of any type it will bring us good luck? Please tell me more about crystals. Thank you. Love, Pat*

Dear Pat

Put your crystal in the south-west for relationships enhancement and in the north-east for personal growth. Not all crystals are equally good. But they seldom do harm, so having crystals around is always a good thing.

# Does pot pourri give out shar chi?

*I read about dried flowers giving out shar chi. Does this include pot pourri? Is pot pourri bad, even in drawers and cupboards? Anonymous*

Dear Anonymous

Pot pourri is not considered to be dried flowers. Only dried flowers (which are dead flowers attempting to look like live flowers) are bad. They give out negative yin energy because they are dead. Pot pourri can be considered a perfume rather than a flower – just like a wooden chair is a chair rather than a dead tree, but a dead tree with no leaves on it standing in your garden is bad. And if you are planning on keeping the pot pourri in drawers and cupboards, well – what is there to worry about?

# Carpet feng shui

*My front door faces east and I am looking for a carpet to put right inside. There are many I Ching symbols available – which would be most auspicious? We live in the desert of Arizona, are retired on fixed incomes and are born under the dog and pig signs. Thank you, Carole*

Dear Carole

Hi there! Place a green carpet at your entrance to enhance the wood element of the east. Best not to place any I Ching symbols, since that would mean stepping on the symbol itself.

# Is red jade bad?

*I love your column and your sage advice. My question involves wearing jade. Does the colour matter? I am a "wood" person – should I wear only green jade? Should I avoid red jade, since red is a colour associated with fire, and fire destroys wood? Is it a bad idea, in general, to wear red jade during the Year of the Hare? Thank you! Evelyn*

Dear Evelyn

The Chinese believe that wearing jade is good for the circulation of chi within the human body, and each of the colours is supposed to be especially good for certain organs of the body. Thus green jade is said to be good for the limbs and other arthritic ailments; red jade is good for the heart and a protection against heart diseases; while white jade is excellent for the head and lung ailments. This is why wearing jade is so popular with the Chinese. Meanwhile, as far as we know, everyone can wear any colour of jade. There are no taboos, and you can wear jade at most times. Going into exactly the years when you should not wear jade is too advanced a form of feng shui, and I myself often disregard this aspect of the practice, as the effect is quite marginal.

## Hanging crystal and windchimes

*Is it auspicious to hang a three-rod metal windchime in the north section of my living room? Someone gave me a crystal shaped like a snowflake with pointed ends – is it also auspicious to hang it and, if so, where should I hang it? Winnie*

Dear Winnie

A three-rod windchime has no significance at all. A snowflake is not a good thing to hang up – it causes poison arrows.

## Releasing my turtles

*I wanted to keep a pair of turtles in the east corner of my living room. However, I only want to keep small ones. Would there be any impact on the feng shui, or on health matters, if I release these two turtles into a nearby public pond and buy myself two new little turtles in two to three years' time? Best regards, Kwa*

Dear Kwa

Nothing wrong with that at all. The only thing is that when you release them, make sure they can survive and fend for themselves... Then bring in another two little ones.

## Silent windchimes

*If you don't have a breeze blowing your chimes, do they do any good? Harvey*

Dear Harvey

Yes, windchimes can do their job of "pressing down" bad luck without them making a single sound. It's the metal and the rods that do the trick.

# Turtle in the north, but it's the kitchen

*I have read several feng shui books, and one regularly mentioned tip is to place a turtle in the northern sector of the house. I have some questions:*

*1. The northern sector of my house is the kitchen. Can I still place a turtle there?*

*2. I have a wood-carved turtle. As the northern sector is represented by the water element, will the wood element of the turtle be suitable in this location?*

*3. If a wood-element turtle is not suitable, what should I get? Would a stone (earth) or metal turtle be all right? (Am I right, as I think a copper/brass turtle is more suitable since metal produces water.)*

*Thanks in advance and best regards, T.C.*

Dear T.C.

Yes, you can place a wood turtle in the north, even if it is the kitchen. But better a real or a ceramic turtle.

# An auspicious amount for a red wedding packet

*A girlfriend of mine is getting married in January next year. Please can you suggest the right amount of ang pau (red packet), so that it will bring good luck to her marriage. Thanks, Lisa*

Dear Lisa

Any number that ends in eight is great: the best are 118, 148, 168 and 188... Just add the zeros – the more, the better of course.

# Dealing with cactus plants

*Hello... Due to our weather in Canada we have to bring in our four cactus plants over the winter. You have said that it is bad feng shui to have cacti indoors. These are dear to my husband, and we have them on top of our bathroom in our studio. Any ideas for balancing the energy from them? Thanks so much! Susie*

Dear Susie

As long as they are not in the bedroom or dining room, I suppose you can live with them during the winter.

# Keeping arrowana fish

*I would really appreciate if you could answer some questions I have about keeping arrowanas in the home. Lillian Too mentions in her book that it is best to keep one or five arrowanas.*
*Questions:*

1. *Is this because of their tendency to fight with each other when numbers between two and four are kept in the same tank, or are the numbers one and five significant?*
2. *I now have one arrowana in my home and would like to get maybe another two, but in separate tanks. What do you think? Best wishes, Ang*

*Lillian Too mentions that one arrowana placed in the north is the most potent remedy.*
*Questions:*

1. *I have my arrowana placed in that location. Unfortunately, there is a lot of human traffic in this area, and this is causing it some grief when someone in my family makes a sudden move. I could move it to my south-east corner, but this location is visible when facing in from the front door. I have read somewhere that it is bad luck to have your arrowana visible when standing outside the front door. Your opinion is greatly appreciated.*
2. *Should I get another arrowana or two, and at which locations should I put the separate tanks? Any problems with putting two in two-tiered tanks?*

*I really could do with your advice here, and thank you in advance for your help. Best regards, Victor*

Dear Ang and Victor

Actually, the best number of arrowanas to keep is one, but keeping five is said to be excellent for creating protection luck, as the arrowanas will "slice through killing chi". Those who like this fish can keep as many as they wish, as long as the house or room is large enough. Too many fish tanks can cause excess water, which can transform good into bad. The best place for the arrowana is in the north, because this is the sector of the water element, but placing it in the south-east is also good. There is nothing wrong with the fish tank being visible from the front door – in fact, it is good luck.

# Crystal balls

*In Lillian Too's books she says that six is the correct number of crystal balls to display, but the shops have seven, arranged in an hexagonal pattern. Which is correct? And what colour should these crystal balls be? Anonymous*

Dear Anonymous

Six is the correct number for the north-west because it represents heaven luck. Seven crystal balls are good for the west corner. The shops probably use seven balls because aesthetically this is more pleasing. So you have to choose whether you want to go for symmetry or for good feng shui. As for the colour, clear (white) quartz crystal is best, but I love crystals, so I collect all sorts of colours.

# Dragon-headed tortoise

*Please could you advise me as to the meaning of the dragon-headed tortoise, as we are unsure. We have just purchased one within the last few days, as we thought it was the figurine that brought good wealth and good health into your home. George and Lisa*

Dear George and Lisa

You are absolutely correct. The dragon tortoise combines the best attributes of both the dragon and the tortoise. It is of course a legendary creature, but it means all the good things that make up a happy and prosperous life. Thus it stands for longevity, protection, courage and uccess. Place this decorative object anywhere in your home, but best in the north, the east and the south-east.

# Where to find feng shui products

*I have just read one of Lillian Too's books, and I have a problem finding some of the stuff she mentions. I would like to buy a pair of three-legged frogs for my living room, and one with the gold coin in its mouth which goes near the door. I can't find the mandarin ducks for love, either, or the Buddha with the coins. I searched all over Chinatown in Manhattan and I had no luck finding any of these items. Janice*

Dear Janice,

Hey, try the on-line stores that we recommend.... Go back to our website: www.wofs.com.

# Instinctive feng shui?

*I am wondering...can feng shui be instinctive? My reason for asking is that sometimes I just get the feeling to buy a certain object or piece of art. For instance, I have been wanting a water fountain in my house for a long time – I just had this inner feeling that I should have one in my house. I have not be able to afford one, but I am saving towards it. I also have this need to mirror the entire wall in my living room, as well as my bedroom (although from what I have read so far, I have to be careful in doing this). Anonymous*

Dear Anonymous

I would not say "No" to your question... Yes, instinct is sometimes quite smart about these things – perhaps it comes from a past life, I don't know. But remember that instinct cannot be taught. It is based on your own consciousness and defies explanation.

# Can I use plain salt water to clean my crystal?

*I just bought some crystals and read in Lillian's book that I have to soak them in sea-salt water for seven days and seven nights. I live in the mountains, so cannot get any sea-water – is plain salt water okay? Anonymous*

Dear Anonymous

No, it must be rock-salt water. You don't need to get fresh sea-water to soak your crystals in. Try your supermarket – most supermarkets sell rock salt. Just dilute this rock salt in water to get your "sea-water".

# Bamboo flutes

*We have many overhead beams in our home, as we have a thatched house. I read that one can hang bamboo fluted with red ribbons on the beams. As I have had no luck in finding bamboo flutes, would ordinary bamboo do? The bamboo is hollow. Should the ends be cut in a slanted manner or just left as they are? Do I hang them only on the beams that go over one's head? Anonymous*

Dear Anonymous

Ordinary bamboo should do the trick...but you should cut the ends to emulate the shape of the flute. What the bamboo flutes do, when hung, is encourage good chi to rise up through the hollow and press up against the bad energy coming down from the exposed beams. Remember to tie your bamboo with red string, because this is what will attract the good chi to the mouth of the flutes.

# Using feng shui enhancers incorrectly?

*My husband (a water rabbit, KUA number 1) went to buy a three-legged toad painted in gold and a pair of pink pigs made of crystal from a crystal shop. He placed both of them in the south of the living hall, facing in. He also checked his fortune at the same shop by taking a photo of his face to see the different types of light around his body. From this, he was advised to purchase one white and one yellow crystal to wear on his chest on a necklace, to improve his wealth and career, which cost him another 200 dollars.*

*Later he was advised to place a pair of fish instead of pigs, according to Sung S.K. (a Hong Kong feng shui master). However, he still followed his original idea of pigs and a toad.*

*The next day his car stalled and that cost him another few hundred dollars to repair. Is there anything wrong with what he purchased, or is it that the items are placed wrongly? The three-legged toad is supposed to bring wealth. Does the toad need to be hidden away, or turned around with its mouth facing the wall and back facing the front during the night, then turned around again during the day? Thank you, Tiffany*

Dear Tiffany

Oh dear, I really don't know what to say. The way you describe it makes me feel that your husband is quite gullible. I think he should listen to the feng shui master and not to the shopkeeper. Fish for wealth I can understand, but pink pigs!! Really! As for the toad...this must be placed near the main door, but not directly in front, as though it is about to leave the house taking all the gold with him!

## Do I need to repeat the ritual?

*I have done the 49-day ritual (as advocated in Lillian Too's books). It ended on the 3 July, but to date nothing has happened. I did, however, do the ritual after midnight on a few occasions and wondered if this was the problem, but I did not skip a day. Would you kindly advise whether I need to be more patient, or do you think I must redo it? Thanks, Jane*

Dear Jane

Try to be relaxed when you do this 49 day ritual – and forget about it after you have done it – otherwise your energies become too anxious which causes them to become negative.

## Chinese coins

*Can you tell me which is the yin and which is the yang face of the Chinese coins? I have been dying to tape three of them to the file that holds all my bank statements. Thanks,*
*Jackie*

Dear Jackie

The four letters are the yang side and the two letters are the yin side. Stick them yang side up. Good luck!

# Dragon ring: which finger?

*Recently I bought a dragon gold ring for my husband. Which finger should he wear it on to enhance his luck? Anonymous*

Dear Anonymous

I would suggest that the ring is worn on any finger he is comfortable with, on the hand that he writes with. The dragon will give his hand much auspicious yang energy.

# Kitty litter box

*I have moved into a three-bedroom apartment that I share with flatmates. However, I also have pets (two cats and one dog). Here is the problem I am currently trying to solve... Where do I place the kitty litter box? We live in the city. I wanted to place it in the bathroom, but my flatmates object. Can you help? Thank you, K.*

Dear K.

Kitty litter boxes are like miniature toilets, and give out the same negative energy. So, just as all feng shui masters will advocate that you minimize the space used and visibility of your toilets, you should do the same for your kitty litter box. You should also ensure that you do not place it in any of the sectors important to you. (I have seen many a time how a toilet in the south-west can destroy any marriage luck coming one's way.) The best solution really is to walk your cats and dog often, so they don't have to poo in your living space at all.

# A successful wish-list

*I wrote my list of wishes 49 times and signed it with my name 49 times, and then I burned it. To my surprise, two days later my wish materialized. Honestly, I really had not expected it to work. I wished to be successful at my job interview – and I was. I wonder if I can start with another list of wishes directly? A big hug from Asa*

Dear Asa

Most certainly you may. You can do the list as many times as you like, but one wish at a time, okay?

# The 49-day ritual

*I have a question about one of Lillian Too's tips. She suggests that for making our wishes come true we should write out a wish-list 49 times, sign it 49 times and do this for 49 days. My questions are as follows:*

1. *How detailed does my wish-list have to be? Can I just write down the names or key words of the things I wish for?*
2. *Is there a limit to what I can wish for?*
3. *How does this affect my spirituality as a committed Christian?*
4. *Can I type a wish-list out each day and then print it off the computer and just sign the page 49 times; or do I have to physically write it out each day?*

*Many thanks, Margaretha*

Dear Margaretha

The wish-list is apparently one example of Taoist magic given to Lillian Too when she was in Hong Kong. She tried using it several times and it worked, hence she decided to share it with her readers. It is apparently important to write it out physically and then sign it 49 times faithfully for 49 days. This engages the mind and causes it to focus strongly and with determination on the wish. Doing it by computer does not work. Also, if you have too many wishes then there is not the same level of determination. As for the religious implication, I would not want to comment.

# Is the colour red for weak metal people?

*I am interested to know whether for those people who are of weak metal element it is still advisable to wear red clothing during auspicious occasions, such as the lunar New Year and one's wedding? Anonymous*

Dear Anonymous

This is an excellent question. Yes, you should wear red during festive occasions to attract auspicious yang energy. Also, each person has eight elements in their basket of elements, and fire may be good as a balancing element. But do not wear too much red too often.

# Feng shui and cars

*I'm new to feng shui, and I'm wondering whether feng shui can be applied to a car? Regards, Jerry*

Dear Jerry

Why? Have you already feng shui'd your house, office and garden, and are now looking for other objects to play with? Or are you just a car freak?

But yes, of course feng shui can be applied to cars. Firstly, there is the question of colour. If your element is wood, say, then you should not get a silver car, because silver represents metal, and metal destroys wood. Instead, a blue car that represents water is auspicious for wood people, because water feeds wood.

Secondly, there is the number plate. The best numbers to have are eights, sixes and nines. Twos and threes, if found together, are pretty bad. Similarly, fives and nines together are bad. If you want to know more about numbers and their feng shui significance, have a look in http://www.lillian-too.com/books.html, or in Lillian Too's book, *Chinese Numerology in Feng Shui*.

Thirdly, there is the model of the car to think about. A Mercedes is good for everyone; a Skoda's good for no one. Get the picture?